All About the Desert

BY SAM AND BERYL EPSTEIN

THERE really is a Timbuktu, and it lies on the southern border of the great Sahara. Its exciting "discovery" by a single bold Frenchman, and his daring trek across 1000 miles of the Sahara, are only a part of the adventure and wonder of this story about deserts. What makes a desert dry? And how do men, beasts and plants live there? Only the brave, the lucky and the specially equipped can survive, and how they do makes fascinating reading. In famous deserts over the globe, Young Readers will meet strange plants and animals, fierce desert tribes whose men never unveil their faces, and primitive Bushmen who can hit a flying bird with a throwing club at 150 feet.

THIS MONTH'S *Allabout Book*

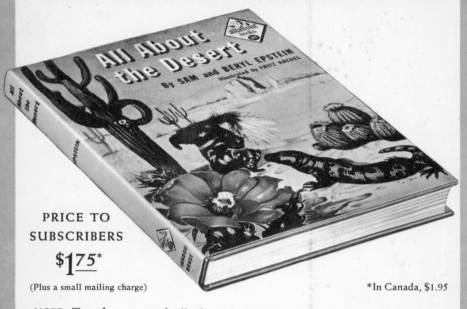

PRICE TO SUBSCRIBERS

$1⁷⁵*

(Plus a small mailing charge)

*In Canada, $1.95

NOTE: To order a copy of *All About the Desert* parents need only fill out and return the attached order card. The book will be sent at once with its own bill.

[PLEASE SEE OTHER SIDE]

FAMOUS PIRATES OF THE NEW WORLD

Famous Pirates of the New World

BY A. B. C. WHIPPLE

Illustrated by Robert Pious

RANDOM HOUSE · NEW YORK

This one is for
ANN

First Printing
© Copyright, 1958, by A. B. C. Whipple
All rights reserved under International and Pan-American Copyright
Conventions. Published in New York by Random House, Inc., and
simultaneously in Toronto, Canada, by Random House of Canada,
Limited.
Library of Congress Catalog Card Number: 58–6189
Manufactured in the United States of America
by H. Wolff, New York

Contents

FAMOUS PIRATES OF THE NEW WORLD

1

When Pirates
Ruled the Sea

If you were to go aboard a ship today at New York and sail down through the Caribbean Sea, probably the worst thing that could happen to you would be a storm that made you a little seasick. The chances are that most of your trip would be one sunny day after another with nothing on the gently rolling azure sea but an occasional cruise ship just like yours.

But imagine for a moment that you are on the Caribbean more than 200 years ago. The sun is shining as brightly; the sea is as gentle and blue. But instead of cruising leisurely in among the islands you are running back to New York with half a dozen chests of silver and gold which you have received from selling a shipload of fine New England rum. There is no other way to get the money back home in the eighteenth century. There are few banks or checks or letters of credit; the only way is to take the money home yourself, hidden in the hold of the ship. And you know that the only way to get it home safely is to sail north as fast as you can. There are others who know this too: the pirates.

Imagine that you are the captain of a little trading sloop. You plot the shortest course you can, through the Straits of Florida, the Windward Passage or the Mona Passage. You order all sail set so long as no gales blow. And you keep a lookout posted in the rigging day and night.

Then, four days out from your last port of call, the lookout calls his alarm. You climb the rigging alongside him and, following the line of his pointing arm, you see it.

The ship stands far off on the horizon. Her masts are barely visible. But in the time it takes to go below for a telescope and climb the rigging again, she has gained. Now and then you can make out a bit of her hull.

In only an hour she can be seen clearly from the deck. Another hour and you can study the clean lines of her racing hull, the rake of her masts, the gun ports along her side. Another hour and your last hopeful doubt is gone. As the ship closes the gap, there is no question. She is a pirate.

Perhaps your little sloop carries a gun in her bow or stern. But it is only useful for driving off native landing parties or scaring away marauders in canoes. It is hopeless to consider using one gun against the heavy armament of a pirate ship.

A black flag ripples to the masthead of the ship. A puff of smoke blows away from her bow. At about the time you hear the cannon, the ball splashes in the water ahead. She has fired across your bow—the signal to give up. As you watch, the ship rounds to, presenting her broadside.

A black flag rippled to the masthead of the ship.

The gun ports are open. The cannon are run out. What do you do?

If you are smart, you turn to your first mate and order your flag lowered in surrender.

It is estimated that this happened as often as half a dozen times a day in the Caribbean area during the years when piracy was at its height. And piracy was at its height in the Caribbean for more than a hundred years. In the late seventeenth century, through the eighteenth century and even into the early years of the nineteenth, pirates swept through the Caribbean and along most of the coast of North America. Sometimes a warship or two of the British or United States Navy went chasing after them, but with little lasting success. There simply were too many pirates.

Not until a pirate-hunting fleet under Commodore David Porter devoted years to sweeping the Caribbean clean, in the 1820's, was piracy finally put down. Until then the skipper of a little trading sloop armed with a small bow-chaser gun and aided by a crew of perhaps two

Two hundred years ago pirates ruled the seas.

or three men and a cabin boy, had no choice. He had to run as fast as his sloop would sail, hoping he would not be discovered by pirates. If he were discovered, he could only give up.

Once in a while some brave and foolhardy

Trading sloops put on full sail to avoid them.

captain tried to fight back or make a dash for it. Almost always he found his sloop rocking under the pirate's broadside. He had barely recovered when the attacker swept alongside, the grappling irons clanked across the gunwales and the sword-waving, pistol-firing, shrieking pirates swarmed aboard. What followed could rarely be called a battle; it was too uneven.

The sloop's captain and crew were soon disarmed and lined up along the rail, with any passengers aboard. If anyone tried to hold back a ring or necklace or bag of money, or if the captain refused to tell where the money was hidden, the torture started. It generally was indescribable. Sometimes, even when everyone co-operated with the pirates, the men were tortured anyway, so they would remember to co-operate next time too. It usually took only an hour or so for the pirates to loot the trading vessel, load their own ship and sail off. Another ship had been raided by the pirates of the Spanish Main.

Why was it called the Spanish Main? Because in even earlier days the Spaniards had claimed most of the land in the Caribbean area. Spanish explorers had discovered most of it. Then explorers and soldiers of fortune from other nations, principally Britain, tried to settle on some of the land, and a long running war broke out. From this war developed the buccaneers, who fought on sea and land, the privateers, who were licensed to take the ships of enemy nations, and finally the pirates. The pirates were neither buccaneers nor privateers; they were plain outlaws of the sea. But they flourished for the next century and more.

They are the men you are about to meet. Not all of them were vicious and cruel, as you will see. Not all of them were always successful. Not all of them, in fact, were men; a few women went a-pirating too. Men and women, they lived in a time when law and order did not rule the sea as it does now. *They* ruled the sea.

Their time will not come again. But while it lasted, this is how it was.

2

The Dark Secret of Captain Flood

Captain James Flood had a secret. He kept it well, so well that when he died his secret almost died with him. In all his life Captain Flood revealed his secret to only one man, the first mate of his pirate ship. If he had not told his first mate, we would not know his strange, evil story. But we do, and here it is—the dark secret of Captain Flood.

He came from Jamaica, one of the major islands of the Caribbean Sea. Nothing else is known about his background. His story has come down to us through a legend of the islands, passed on by generation after generation. No one has ever found out what kind of life he led as a child, or how he came to be a pirate. All that anyone knows is that his pirate ship suddenly appeared in the Caribbean in the early years of the eighteenth century. The ship's name, the *Shark*, was well chosen, because Captain Flood was one of the most bloodthirsty pirates of the Spanish Main.

He was also one of the smartest. The *Shark* was a small sloop, but that did not keep Captain Flood from attacking the great 30-gun French frigate *L'Oriflamme* one night. He found her in the harbor of Petit Goâve, at the western end of the island of Hispaniola, the area now known as Haiti.

Captain Flood sailed up to the harbor entrance in the dark of the night. Inside the harbor he could see the lights of his prize as she lay tied to a wharf. Two boats slid away from the *Shark*, their oars muffled with cloth to prevent any splashing. The faces of the men were blackened to hide them in the darkness. Silently they rowed into the harbor and under the towering stern of the big French frigate.

Luck was with Captain Flood and his men that black night. The big frigate's guns were unmanned. Most of the crew were ashore. Only one watchman paced the wide deck. It took scarcely more than a few minutes for Flood's men to slip up behind the sailor, put a knife into him and kill him before he could cry out the warning. His body still lay on the deck of the French frigate as the pirates cast off the lines, shook out her mainsail and swung her away from the wharf.

There were other watchmen in the harbor, and big guns guarded the entrance. But so swiftly and silently did Flood's men work that no one saw the frigate's tall masts sweep across the bay and out to the open sea.

As the ship caught the wind in the rest of her sails outside the harbor, she picked up speed. Captain Flood, who had waited aboard the *Shark* near the harbor entrance, now sent her after his prize. Together the two vesseis

Silently they rowed under the stern of the frigate.

swept out into the Windward Passage, between the islands of Hispaniola and Cuba. There Flood went aboard the frigate and ordered his men to undo the locks they had clamped on her hatches. The sailors below were hauled on deck, a few at a time, and invited to join the crew of pirates. Some accepted. The rest were put over the side into two of the frigate's boats, to row off over the horizon to shore if they could.

They did, finding a beach at Cape Tiburon, on the western tip of Hispaniola. But apparently these were the last victims of Captain Flood to live to tell the tale.

In fact, in the next battle even some of Flood's own pirates were sacrificed. The *Shark* and the captured frigate, which Flood had renamed *Le Moustique* (*The Mosquito*), had crossed the Atlantic Ocean looking for prizes. Off the island of Madeira they attacked a huge, heavily armed East Indiaman. This time Flood tried a frontal attack. And it failed. But he was still too smart to pay for his mistake. He sent the little *Shark* in against the huge ship but stayed out of range himself in his frigate. The *Shark* was pounded to pieces. If Flood had attacked with both his ships, he might have won the battle. Evidently the captain of the East Indiaman thought so. At least he ran off as soon as he had shot up the *Shark* enough to outdistance her. Waiting out of range aboard his frigate, Flood watched his prize go without trying to catch her. Then he went over to the *Shark* and transferred all her treasure and able-bodied men to his frigate.

The injured he simply left aboard the sinking *Shark*. As he sailed away, the men aboard the frigate could hear the screams of the wounded on the *Shark*, unable to escape the water slowly creeping over them.

Now there was only the frigate. Back across the Atlantic she sailed, this time to the Bahamas, a string of islands and keys off the east coast of Florida. And in among the Bahamas, Captain Flood and his crew had a remarkable run of luck.

In fact, so many prizes did *Le Moustique* capture that within a few weeks her hold was loaded down with gold and jewels and coins. Captain Flood began to worry about the frigate. How could she maneuver well in battle, with her hull settled so low in the water?

That was when he dreamed up his secret. That was also when he told the one man with whom he shared his secret, his first mate. Little is known about this man except his nickname, "Caesar." Flood had no choice but to bring Caesar into his plot, because he could not handle it all by himself.

He had made his preparations, though. For many years he had searched out the loneliest islands of the Caribbean, going ashore on one after another until he had found just the island he had wanted. He now set the course of the pirate ship for this spot—Lotus Island, off the east coast of Hispaniola.

This end of Hispaniola is now the Dominican Republic, and the island is now Catalina. Then it was a wild and desolate place, the home of nothing more than a few goats, some great lumbering turtles and thousands of sea birds wheeling and squawking over the island's steep cliffs.

The birds swirled angrily about the intruding frigate as she eased through the narrow passage into the harbor. It was noon when *Le Moustique* swung to her anchor in the deepest part of the bay. And all that afternoon the boats went back and forth to the shore. They carried the chests of silver and gold and jewels to be buried in the dense jungle back of the beach. By sundown the work was done, and the rum was broken out for the celebration.

For most of that night raucous laughter and singing echoed across the bay as the pirates celebrated their good luck. It was nearly dawn when the last man had fallen into a dead sleep, and the ship rode quietly at her anchor with no one stirring aboard. Now it was time for Captain Flood and First Mate Caesar to go to work.

While Caesar got a boat ready, Flood hoisted up three chests which he had carefully hidden in his cabin. The two men lowered the chests into the boat, climbed down and pushed off, rowing toward the highest cliff on the shore.

It seemed to rise straight into the sky from the beach, where rocks and coral ledges showed above the low tide. Around the side of the great cliff, the jungle crowded down to the water's edge. There was one break in the wall of trees and underbrush, where a stream trickled into the bay. Flood and Caesar made for this spot.

As the boat grounded on the pebbles of the beach, the two men jumped out and lifted the chests onto the bank. Then came the difficult part.

There was of course no way up the face of the cliff. But back in the jungle behind the beach there was a path. It was not much more than a faint trail worn many years before, probably by some of the herds of goats which roamed about the island. It was narrow and blocked in many places by vines and underbrush. As it climbed the hill, it became steep, twisting and dangerous. But Flood and Caesar made it to the top, lugging one of the chests with them. Down the back of the cliff they went. Twice more they staggered up the steep trail, lifting and dragging the other two chests with them. It was almost noon by the time they had the last chest on the

Two more times they staggered up the steep trail.

peak of the cliff. They rested, wiping the sweat from their faces and necks, swatting at the insects that swarmed around them in clouds, and looking out across the bay that stretched away from them far below.

Captain Flood rose and walked over to a tiny

cave back of the edge of the cliff. He poked about in the cave and came out with a block and tackle—a pulley which was caked with rust and loops of what seemed like miles of rope. After some yanking and grunting, he had the pulley working again. He fastened it to a stubby tree which grew at the cliff's edge. He tied one end of the rope to the first chest and swung it over the ledge.

Slowly, with the rope creaking through the rusted pulley, the chest went down the sheer side of the cliff. About halfway down, it rested on a tiny ledge. This was the only place where the cliff did not appear to be like the side of a wall, going straight down hundreds of feet to the coral ledges and rocks which now looked so small, far below them. Here and there a bush stuck out of the cliffside, but there were no other ledges. This one was directly below the edge of the cliff where Flood and Caesar stood; and as they watched, the first chest came to rest on it.

Flood tied down the end of the rope which he had been paying out. One after the other he and Caesar slid down the rope and landed on the ledge. Cut into the side of the cliff was a fair-sized cave. Together the men untied the chest and shoved it into the cave. Then, at Flood's direction, Caesar climbed back up the rope, hand over hand. He pulled up the rope, tied it to the second chest and lowered it slowly to the ledge where Flood waited. Sliding down after it, he helped Flood push it into the cave. Once more he pulled himself hand over hand back up to the top of the cliff. He tied on the third chest and lowered it to Flood. Sliding down the rope, he helped the captain hide this last chest.

So it was that Captain Flood and his first mate hid away for themselves the choicest part of the pirate ship's loot. In those three chests they had a treasure worth perhaps more than all the gold and silver and jewels they had buried in the jungle the day before. The rest of the crew would know nothing about it. Whenever they wanted, Flood and Caesar could return, help themselves to whatever they needed and be rich for the rest of their lives.

But that was not all of Captain Flood's secret.

The two men had stuffed their pockets with gold and were about to climb back up the rope, when Flood looked out across the bay and shouted, "The ship! Look!"

Thereupon Caesar made his mistake. He turned his back to Flood as he looked across the bay. At the same moment that he saw the ship riding quietly and safely at anchor, he was pushed off the ledge.

Caesar had time only to wave his arms in the air and scream before he was gone. Captain Flood leaned back against the cliffside, panting and listening. The scream died in a crashing thud. Flood waited a moment to catch his breath, then grabbed the rope and climbed hand over hand to the top of the cliff.

After he had hidden the block and tackle, he looked over the edge to see if Caesar's body was in sight. It was not—only the jagged coral ledges and rocks could be seen, with the water snarling among them.

It had worked exactly as Captain Flood had planned. Now he had the treasure of the three chests to himself. He would have to explain to the crew that Caesar had fallen into the water and drowned. But once he had done that, the three rich chests would be all his, and no one would know the murder he had committed to keep them to himself. That was Captain Flood's secret.

He did convince his crew. The few who were awake when he returned to the ship believed his story. With no questions asked, Flood ordered the anchor up. *Le Moustique* rode the tide out of the bay and into the open sea.

Then, strangely, Captain Flood's luck turned against him. It took a while for him to know it. But after a few weeks he began to realize that no matter where he went there were no prizes to be had. It was as if the Caribbean had been swept clean of merchant ships.

Captain Flood took *Le Moustique* out onto the Atlantic. Still no luck. He decided to give his men a much-needed vacation, and put into the harbor at New Providence, the beautiful island now called Nassau. Then it was the rough,

tough, brawling frontier town of the Caribbean.
Flood's men could hardly wait to swarm ashore.

It took them only a few days to spend everything they had not buried—days which Captain
Flood spent out in the harbor aboard the frigate, fretting to be away. He was not going to
take the chance of liquor loosening his tongue
in one of those waterfront taverns. The secret
was all his now; he shared it with no one. So
he spent his time in the loneliness of his cabin,
itching to haul up anchor and sail away.

When finally his men had returned aboard
ship, exhausted and penniless, all agreed that it
was time to return to Lotus Island and dig up
those chests. A few days later *Le Moustique* was
again slipping slowly into the almost landlocked
bay. The anchor had hardly taken hold in the
harbor bottom when the crew was crashing
through the jungle to the hiding place of their
loot.

The chests were still there and still heavy.
They were brought back to the ship, and the
rusted locks were broken open. The gold had
turned green; the silver was black with tarnish;

the jewels were covered with a slimy mold. But all were as valuable as before, and the men chattered excitedly about the heaps of treasure as they thought again of those taverns and gaming tables of New Providence.

Later when the pirates were in a deep sleep, Flood dropped a boat over the side. By the faint light of a rising moon, he started rowing for the shore. As he rowed, he looked over his shoulder at the great cliff rising into the sky above him, black and menacing.

By the time the boat crunched onto the shore, Flood was so excited that he set out on the run for the path behind the cliff. He was panting heavily when he reached the top, but he did not wait to rest before digging into the little cave for the block and tackle. It was there, apparently untouched. He quickly rigged it to the tree stump and swung himself off the edge, dropping hand over hand to the tiny ledge halfway down the cliff.

The chests were still in the cave, jammed with gold and jewels and precious stones. Captain Flood fondled them greedily and stuffed his pockets with all he could carry. From inside his shirt he pulled a bag, which he filled with more loot and hung around his neck, buttoning his shirt over it again. It would be impossible for him to shove the chest out onto the ledge and haul it to the top of the cliff by himself. He had to be satisfied with what his pockets and the bag would carry. He took a last loving look at what he was leaving behind until the next visit, closed the chests and went out of the cave.

The ledge was bathed in the light of the moon, which now hung out over the bay. The whole island lay beneath him, with a fringe of white sand shining between the jungle and the water's edge. The ripples of the harbor glinted in the moonlight and the dark hulk of the ship squatted in the middle of the bay. Captain Flood stood admiring the sight for a moment and then reached for the rope.

It was gone.

For a minute or two he fumbled about, not realizing what had happened. But then he heard a sound that made his blood run cold. It started like a low chuckle, rising into a cackling laugh.

But it was more the hysterical cry of a madman.

Somehow Flood knew, even before he looked to the top of the cliff, what was silhouetted against the moonlit sky. He was right. There was no mistaking the outline of the head. It was Caesar.

What Flood could not understand was how it had happened. How had Caesar lived? How could anyone have fallen off that ledge and survived? In a mad, gloating singsong, Caesar explained. He had struck against a bush growing out of the side of the cliff. He had bounced into a spreading tree at the bottom. He had broken an arm and a leg in the fall, and he had been knocked unconscious. But the bush and the tree had saved his life. The rising tide had brought him to, and he had dragged himself up onto the beach beside the foot of the cliff. And then, as if sent by Providence, a merchantman had put into the harbor for wood and water and had rescued him. He had pretended to be a marooned sailor and had been taken to Kingston, Jamaica, with no further questions.

It had taken Caesar a few months to recover.

Captain Flood scooped up masses of jewels and coins.

But as soon as he was well again, he had shipped out on another merchantman and had deserted at San Domingo. There he had hired a sloop and made his way back to Lotus Island. He had had to wait for more months than he could remember. But through it all, he had known that there was one thing of which he could be sure. Captain Flood would return to the island and to the cave on the ledge. Now he had. Caesar laughed again—a laugh that brought goose flesh to Captain Flood's skin.

But despite his mad cackle, Caesar had a plan, which he now offered to Flood. It was a scheme which he had thought out during the many months while he had waited and nursed his revenge. If Flood would fasten the rope to each of the three chests, one by one, Caesar would then let down the rope for a fourth time for Flood—after he had hidden the chests.

Flood did not reply immediately. He settled down on the ledge to consider some other way out. After what he had done to Caesar, he could expect the same kind of treatment. Once he had helped Caesar hoist the three chests to the top of the cliff, he would be left to starve. Flood decided to wait until dawn, which he estimated was about three hours off. Perhaps he could find a way of escape from the ledge.

So he waited, while the moon slowly crossed the sky, while the pirate frigate below him swung around on her anchor with the changing tide, and while the muffled, impatient stamping of Caesar could be heard above him. In the stillness of the night, Flood could hear the water sucking angrily among the jagged coral formations below. Far off in the jungle behind the cliff a bird shrieked in the night. Out at sea the moon glinted off a breaker. Thus the hours dragged by.

The faint light of dawn had just begun to spread across the sky when the whole harbor seemed to explode. Below, in the middle of the bay, the pirate ship suddenly erupted in one great ball of flame. Probably a drunken crewman had lit a match in the powder magazine. Whatever the cause, *Le Moustique* blew into bits that soared into the air and fell hissing back into the water. One minute the frigate lay quietly at anchor; the next minute she was nothing more than a few big chunks of wood burning to the water's edge. As the last flame was quenched, Flood searched the moonlit water for a sign of some survivor swimming for the shore. There was none.

With the full light of dawn, he studied the bay more carefully. Except for a charred timber or two, it was as if there had been no ship in the harbor a few hours before.

And now that there was light, Flood looked for a way up or down from his ledge. He could find nothing but sheer precipice, broken only here and there by a projecting bush or stub of a tree.

Then he thought of a plan. It was desperate, almost suicidal. But it was the only way.

Looking up, he saw that Caesar's head had disappeared from the edge of the cliff. A call brought him back. Flood said that he gave up. He was ready to tie on the chests if Caesar would send down the rope. He agreed that all three chests belonged to Caesar.

He had barely finished his promise when the

block and tackle creaked and the rope started swinging down toward the ledge. Meanwhile, Flood climbed back into the cave and hauled out the first chest. The rope was waiting for him when he emerged.

He grabbed the rope, wound it around the chest, tied it firmly, tested the knot and yelled to Caesar to haul away. The line went taut. The chest bumped along the ledge and swung away. As it swung back toward Flood, it was at about shoulder height. Flood took a breath and jumped for it.

Apparently Caesar was too busy hauling the rope to realize that he had a double load. Perhaps he figured that only now had the chest swung free. In any case, the combined weight of the chest and Flood, who now hung onto the rope at the bottom, was almost more than the tackle and the tree trunk could bear. There was a creaking and a snapping, but somehow everything held. Gradually the chest, with Captain Flood still out of sight below it, rose alongside the sheer face of the cliff.

Inch by inch it came to the top. Sweating and

swearing, Caesar hauled away until he had it high enough to swing in toward him. That was when he spotted Flood.

In dumb amazement he let the rope slip through his hands. At the same moment Flood jumped again, this time swinging himself the few inches to the edge of the cliff, where he grabbed hold of a rock and hung there. The chest, missing him by little more than an inch, plummeted past his shoulders.

Caesar caught himself and grabbed at the rope. It was whirring too fast through the tackle. He tried to take a turn around the tree stump. The rope jerked free. Seconds later the crash echoed up the side of the cliff as the chest struck the rocks below.

The two panting men stared at each other. Flood tried to haul himself up over the rock, but he was too exhausted for the moment. Now Caesar came slowly and menacingly toward him.

He tried to stomp Flood's fingers loose. He mashed one, but Flood managed to shift his hand out of the way in time to save the others.

Caesar then raised his boot, took careful aim and brought it down on Flood's head.

In the same moment Flood ducked and reached out with one hand. He caught Caesar by the ankle.

Kicking angrily, Caesar tried to free himself. But Flood was hanging on for his life. Caesar could only grab at a bush, haul himself away from the edge and watch his enemy come slowly up after him. Then, as Flood let go and clambered to his feet, Caesar plunged at him. The two men went into a clinch and wrestled at the brink of the cliff, silently, desperately, murderously. Then it was over.

Flood reeled back, seemed to hang in mid-air for a moment, flailing his arms. Then he was gone.

Caesar lay on the grass away from the edge of the cliff for fully half an hour before he could recover his strength. Without looking over the side, he secreted the block and tackle for a future visit. Carefully he made his way down the narrow trail on the back side of the cliff and climbed over the rocks to where the mashed corpse of Captain Flood lay wedged between two coral shelves. The clothes had been ripped from the body, but Caesar found some of the best jewels scattered near by. He stuffed them in his pockets. The bag around Flood's neck had broken open. It was still usable though. The remains of the chest lay a few hundred feet away. From the jumble of doubloons and silver pieces, Caesar selected the best and filled the bag. He did not look back at the body, already being submerged by the rising tide, as he picked his way back to the beach.

He could not recall, as he told the story later, how many weeks he had to wait before a passing ship spotted his distress signal flying atop the great cliff. But again he was lucky, and again he was rescued within a few weeks from the time he had fashioned his signal. In those few weeks the tides and the ravenous fish had wiped out all evidence of Captain Flood.

Caesar of course said nothing then about the hidden chests or the dramatic fight on the top of the cliff. Many years later he made his way back to Lotus Island. The chests were gone.

Then he told his story. No one ever did find out who made off with the chests. But even today, when heavy winds drive the tide far out of the bay, the natives of the island can sometimes pick up a few pieces that still remain of the rich, once-secret treasure of Captain Flood.

3

Blackbeard

Captain James Flood spent most of his life protecting his big secret. Throughout his career one thing was all-important: to keep the course of his voyages, his activities, even his name hidden from those he robbed. He was the perfect example of the kind of pirate who believed that the less known about him the better the chances for continued success. Pirates like Captain Flood were the kind who believed in the famous saying, "Dead men tell no tales."

But there was another kind of pirate in those days. This second kind believed that the more he got talked about, the better. If his name were known all up and down the Atlantic coast as a bloodthirsty pirate, that merely made the job a little easier. If he captured a merchant ship and everyone aboard was already terrified at the mention of his name, he could count on a richer haul. And there was a lot less trouble about it—nobody making a brave, foolish show of defiance. Captain, crew and passengers simply handed over the bullion, jewelry and other treasure they had aboard. In a matter of a few hours the pirate was on his way again. This kind of operator preferred a slogan which became popular two and a half centuries later: "It pays to advertise."

And if ever there were a prime example of this kind of pirate, it was the one who remained the best-advertised for more than 250 years. His name was Blackbeard.

Of course it was not his real name. In fact, nobody knew his real name. Most people said it was Edward Teach, though there were some who said it was Thatch, or Tache. He adopted his nickname because he figured that it would strike terror into the hearts of all who met him. And before he was through, the name "Blackbeard" did just that.

It was a terrifying name partly because of the way Blackbeard suited himself to it. He grew one of the thickest beards ever seen in history. It covered nearly all of his face; no one could tell where his beard stopped and the great lion's mane covering his head and his neck began. About all that could be seen of his face were a huge twisted nose and bulging bloodshot eyes, set off by juglike ears. The beard and hair were usually matted, since he used them for wiping his hands while eating or fighting.

Of course he never actually washed his hands, as anyone could see at a glance. They were not just dirty; they were caked and creased with grime. His clothes were little better, pinned or tied together where they had been torn, streaked with garbage and slime and blood.

Blackbeard tried hard to look repulsive, and anyone who got a close look at him had to admit that he succeeded.

So it was not surprising that his name became hated and feared from the coast of New England to the southernmost island in the Caribbean Sea, which was about the extent of Blackbeard's activities. And it was not surprising to see the horrified reactions of the crew and passengers of a ship when a black flag flew to the masthead of a pursuing ship and the word was whispered down the rail: *Blackbeard.*

His usual method of boarding a ship was to make his appearance even more impressive by sticking slow-burning matches in his hair and lighting them. The matches of Blackbeard's time were like the wick on a bomb or stick of dynamite today. They made a sizzling, crackling sound and filled the air with sulfur fumes.

In those days sailors were very superstitious, and the sight of Blackbeard with his bulging, red-veined eyes, his filthy beard wagging about and those matches burning in his hair, was

Slow-burning matches sizzled in his filthy beard.

enough to convince many a poor sailor that it was the Devil himself.

Not often, but once in a while some passenger not paralyzed with fear would hesitate to part with a ring. Blackbeard settled any such argument with one chop of his cutlass: off came ring, finger and all. Another victim would always have a stunted hand to remind him not to argue with Blackbeard again. And anyone who saw it and asked would spread the word that a pirate named Blackbeard was not to be fooled with. A little here, a little there; it all added up to make Blackbeard the most infamous pirate of all time and the most successful.

It had not always been so easy for him. Ned Teach (if that was his real name) had grown up in the streets of Bristol, England, where he had been a starving orphan. He finally escaped by shipping out as a cabin boy on a vessel bound for the West Indies. There he deserted and set out to make his career. He quickly found that in those days in the wild frontier of the New World he could make a fortune a lot faster as a lawbreaker.

One of the up-and-coming desperados of the West Indies was a tough old pirate named Ben Hornigold. Always on the alert for the young criminals of his time, Hornigold spotted Ned as a likely prospect and took him on as an apprentice. His trust was well founded. Ned proved to be one of the cruelest attackers and dirtiest fighters it had been Hornigold's pleasure to watch in action. A crack shot, Ned could pick off a small child on a merchantman's deck 100 yards away on a tossing sea. And when the pirates swarmed onto the victim's deck, the cutlass-swinging, belly-sticking, eye-gouging tactics of Ned Teach were a sight to see.

But Ben Hornigold was a wise enough old pirate to realize that he had better enjoy the sight while he could; the lad was too good to be an apprentice for long. Hornigold was right. Within only a few months his pupil announced that he wanted to strike out on his own. Hornigold knew he could not stop him if he wanted to, so he gave the young man his blessing.

That was when Teach took the name of Blackbeard. He set out to make the name despised everywhere, and it soon was. The more ships he captured, the more his name was feared and the easier his next capture. The more loot he took, the more men tried to join his crew, so he had the pick of the pirate crews all through the Caribbean. And as ship after ship surrendered to him, he kept the best ones, putting his victims over the side in small boats and substituting his own prize crews. He soon had a pirate fleet, roaming the West Indies and up the Atlantic coast all the way to Maine and Nova Scotia. Back on New Providence Island (the one named Nassau today), which was the headquarters of all the pirates, old Ben Hornigold, who had once been Blackbeard's tutor, was reduced to bragging that he had known the great man when.

The records show that in the spring of 1717, Blackbeard sailed out of New Providence harbor for the last time. His ship, the *Queen Anne's Revenge,* was headed on a long roundabout cruise. It would take Blackbeard to Honduras, to the Carolinas, to New England, back to a lonely harbor on the Carolina coast—and to the bloodiest pirate battle in history.

On the run down to Honduras, Blackbeard met Stede Bonnet. Here was a wealthy planter from Barbados, who had given up his mansion, his wife and his riches to go a-pirating. Besides, Bonnet was the unlikeliest pirate of his times—a landsman who went into battle in an embroidered waistcoat.

Blackbeard rarely sailed in company with other pirates whom he met along the way. Unlike most pirate captains, he ran a taut ship; in fact, he ran a taut fleet. That is, he permitted no nonsense about anyone running the ship but himself. While it was pirate tradition for the crew to vote any captain out of office whenever they wanted to, no one had the courage to suggest any such idea aboard Blackbeard's ship. They realized that there was no one who could bring them half so many prizes. But that was only part of it. They realized even more keenly that the first man to suggest a vote aboard the *Queen Anne's Revenge* would get a cutlass in his belly.

Blackbeard saw to it that his men always remembered this. And he did not intend to have them reminded of more democratic conditions aboard other pirate ships. So Blackbeard's fleet nearly always went its own way.

It was generally understood that pirates did not battle among themselves. They saved their efforts for the merchantmen which were less heavily armed and more easily taken. But Stede Bonnet was too much for Blackbeard to pass up. He calmly took Bonnet prisoner and sent one of his lieutenants aboard Bonnet's ship to sail it in company with his own.

Bonnet did not take kindly to this, of course. But there was nothing he could do about it. And it turned out that while he was Blackbeard's forced guest, the fleet had a very successful cruise. Blackbeard graciously doled out some of the loot to Bonnet's crew. Cruising the Caribbean, they swung north into the Atlantic and up to Bath (then Bath Town), North Carolina. Somewhere in that area—treasure hunters are still trying to find out exactly where—they buried some of the bulging loot. Then they were off again, with Stede Bonnet still aboard Blackbeard's ship.

Again they went south, down among the heavy ship traffic threading through the Florida

Strait and the islands of the West Indies. In only a few weeks the holds were full again, and Blackbeard headed north for Bath Town. But this time he hove to off the harbor of Charleston (then Charles Town), South Carolina. At that time it was one of the busiest ports on the North American coast, and Blackbeard lay in wait for a while to see what he could snap up.

The first nine ships to come out of or approach the harbor were quickly captured. The ninth presented a golden opportunity. She carried $6,000 in coin, to which Blackbeard helped himself. She also carried among her passengers one Samuel Wragge, a member of the South Carolina Governor's Council. The possibilities for ransom were obvious.

Blackbeard sent a note into the city, threatening to send along Samuel Wragge's head if the governor did not pay a ransom within forty-eight hours. He also promised to bring his fleet (then numbering three big ships and two small ones) into the harbor and bombard the city. And instead of demanding thousands of dollars,

Blackbeard asked only for two chests of medicine.

Ever since then historians have tried to figure out why he asked for so little. Perhaps a great number of his men were sick. This was before everyone knew that fruit juices prevented scurvy. Sometimes the entire crew of a ship would be laid low by the disease. Perhaps, as has recently been suggested, Blackbeard was a drug addict and wanted the laudanum in the medicine chests. Perhaps there was no more room for loot in the holds of the fleet, and all Blackbeard needed was a couple more medicine chests. Probably it amused him to terrorize an entire city for so small a ransom. Whatever the reason, he did not have any trouble getting the chests. With a great show of honesty, he handed over the governor's councilman and sailed north.

At this point, for no apparent reason either, Blackbeard told Stede Bonnet he could leave. Bonnet left. Then Blackbeard tried a neat little trick on most of his crew. Sailing two of the ships onto a sand bank, he left them with their crews and went off over the horizon in his own ship, together with his particular cronies in the crew. It happened, too, that nearly all of the loot from the cruise was in his ship.

Into Bath Town they went again, to be received as hospitably as before. Blackbeard had a very profitable arrangement at Bath Town, an arrangement with none other than the Governor of North Carolina, Charles Eden. For a small percentage, which still amounted to a great deal even for a governor in those days, Eden helped Blackbeard sell off his loot. With such help Blackbeard quickly got rid of his latest haul at very good prices and set out again. The cruise which followed was a long one, taking him as far north as New England, then down into the West Indies and out into the Atlantic to Bermuda. Running back to the Carolina coast, Blackbeard slipped through one of the inlets in the great arm of islands sweeping out to Cape Hatteras. He picked Ocracoke Inlet, and rounded into the quiet, hidden harbor on the inside of the island. There he anchored for a long stay, to rest and recuperate and presumably to hide some of his treasure in this secluded spot.

In behind Ocracoke Inlet Blackbeard had a wild celebration. No doubt he felt that he had good reason for it. He had had a very profitable cruise, taking one ship after another with practically no resistance offered by any of them. It seemed as if the Atlantic had been swarming with ships just for his picking. And the prizes had been richer than any in previous years.

But there were a few circumstances which Blackbeard did not realize. Probably he would not have believed them if one of his men had tried to tell him. The reason he had had such a profitable cruise was that most of the other pirates had already been cleaned out. New Providence, Philadelphia, New York City and Newport were no longer the strongholds of piracy they once had been. As a result, merchant skippers felt more secure and were taking greater amounts of coined money abroad with them. That was why Blackbeard had done so well. While his hiding place seemed secure, he did not realize that it was one of the last few places along the North American coast where a pirate could hide out.

Blackbeard had sufficient warning, but he ignored it. One of his men pointed out that if a pursuer came in through Ocracoke Inlet at the right tide, they would have to fight their way out. If they lost that battle, he warned, they would all fry in Hell. Blackbeard's answer was a devilish practical joke. "Come, let us make a Hell of our own," he said, "and try how long we can bear it."

The few men who said they would just as soon be excused from this experiment found themselves rolling head over heels down the deck. All trooped below to the stifling hold. There Blackbeard ordered brimstone pots lighted. In a few minutes the smoke had every-one coughing and crying. Tears rolled from Blackbeard's eyes too, but he gave no sign of having had enough. Finally, after half of his men had suffocated, the weaker members gave up and broke into the open, choking and gasping in the pure air on deck. Blackbeard was the last to lumber up the gangway, coughing and weeping but commenting freely on his crew's lack of preparation for the place to which all of them were doomed.

And indeed it seemed that they were. The messenger bearing the news arrived only a few days after they had dropped anchor in the harbor. The report he brought was that the Governor of Virginia, Alexander Spottswood, had at last had enough from the pirates. In defiance of North Carolina's Governor Eden, Spottswood had sent out an expedition against Blackbeard. Two sloops, commanded by a fire-eating young lieutenant of the Royal Navy named Robert Maynard and manned by crews totaling fifty-five sailors, were already running down the coast toward Ocracoke Inlet. They knew exactly where Blackbeard was anchored, and they intended to come right in after him.

Here Blackbeard made his biggest strategic error. He refused to be the least bit concerned by this news. His reaction was: let them come and get him if they could. In fact, the night after he got the news, he held the biggest

Blackbeard crossed pistols under the table and fired.

party of all. And after a few mugs of rum he pulled off one of his weirdest practical jokes. As he and a few of his men sat around a table in his cabin, Blackbeard suddenly leaned forward, blew out the lamp, crossed two pistols under the table and fired.

One bullet plunked into the cabin bulkhead. The other shattered the kneecap of Blackbeard's first mate, Israel Hands. Picking himself up from the corner where he had sprawled, Hands tried to hold back the gush of blood. To his pained, puzzled question Blackbeard replied with a roar of laughter. "If I don't kill somebody now and then," he shouted, "you'll forget who I am."

Maybe it was because of Blackbeard's own heedlessness; maybe it was because someone went to sleep. But on the afternoon of November 21, 1718, no one noticed the sails of the two sloops of war as Lieutenant Robert Maynard and fifty-five sailors headed straight for Ocracoke Inlet.

Maynard reached the inlet in time to work his way through before the tide turned against him. Once through the narrow passageway, he swung about and sailed up Pamlico Sound toward the harbor where Blackbeard lay in his hide-out. By the time Blackbeard had seen the sloops and realized what had happened, he was trapped.

But he was not caught yet. And as the sun settled across the bay, behind the masts of the sloops of war, both pursuer and pursued made ready for the morning. The tide that now left the harbor full of shoals would then come flooding back into Ocracoke Harbor. With it would come Lieutenant Maynard and his sloops of war.

It seemed like a short night; there was so much to do. Powder, balls and scrap shot had to be stacked near the guns. Blankets were made ready to be soaked over the side, so they could be hung around the powder magazine or used to smother fires. Pistols and cutlasses were piled at the battle stations. Matting was laid along the rail, for many a man had been killed in a sea battle by huge splinters of rail flying through the air. And boats went ashore for loads of sand to spread on the deck, so the men would be able to keep their footing in the blood.

Then they tried to get a few hours' sleep. There was little time left and no sleep. Instead everyone aboard the sloops shifted and turned in his hammock, his stomach churning as he thought of the morning. And aboard the pirate ship the men could ponder on the warning which had been ignored, and the fact that they had finally been run to ground.

Blackbeard slept soundly, dead drunk. By dawn, though, he was fully awake. He had a raging headache and the disposition of a wounded bear. He was never more ready for a good fight.

As he and his men watched, the masts of the two sloops of war came slowly around the high-domed sand banks at the mouth of the harbor. They were riding the tide in before Blackbeard could catch the morning breeze and sail out into the open water of Pamlico Sound. It was going to be close-in fighting. That was all right with Blackbeard. Close-in fighting was his specialty.

The sun rose slowly in the sky, seeming to move faster than the creeping sloops of war. Blackbeard made a last inspection of the deck. Gun ports were opened. Sponges were wetted. Blankets were hung around the powder mag-

azine. Pistols were primed. The smoke from
the slow matches at the guns rose softly in
the still morning air. The men, tense and shak-
ing but ready, stood at their stations. Blackbeard
strode back to his position near the helm. Au-
tomatically he rasped a hardened thumb against
the razor edge of his cutlass. He was ready
too. The fancy lieutenant and his sailor boys
had trapped him in his hole, all right. But
now they had to come in and get him.

As the two sloops rounded into view and
came at him, Blackbeard tried to get the meas-
ure of his enemy. How good a sailor was this
Lieutenant Maynard? Did he have a pilot who
knew the twisting channels and the shoals of
this little harbor? Was there a chance to slip
past the two sloops and into open water? Would
he have to fight off the combined crews of
two war vessels on his own deck? As he watched
and tried to figure it all out, the maneuvering
of the sloops seemed to provide an answer.

One kept her course, straight for the pirate
ship. The other wore off and headed for a point
down the harbor, apparently with the intention

of blocking Blackbeard's escape. This tactic told Blackbeard what he wanted to know—the attackers had no pilot with them, or they would not be trying that trick. They were headed for a sand bar concealed just below the surface of the water.

At Blackbeard's shouted signal the men hoisted anchor and loosed sail. The pirate ship slowly gathered way. While Lieutenant Maynard and his sailors, and even some of Blackbeard's men, watched with surprise, Blackbeard grabbed the helm and headed his ship over toward the beach. Then, just as she seemed about to go aground, he swung her gently around so she ran parallel to the shore. The sloop of war, running down to cut her off, suddenly stopped as if she had reached the end of a rope. With a creaking, grinding lurch she piled onto the sand bar. Howling with glee, Blackbeard sailed down past her, between the bar and the shore, and on toward the harbor mouth and the open sound. Far astern of him, trying to round the sand bar at the other end, Lieutenant Maynard was perfectly outmaneuvered.

But apparently this was too easy for Blackbeard. He simply could not slip out of the grasp of the two sloops like that, without one good parting shot. As he swept past the nearest sloop, he ordered all sail loosed long enough for his guns to be brought to bear. In one thundering broadside he reduced the sloop to near wreckage.

That was when he discovered that he should have resisted the temptation. For at this crucial moment the breeze died.

If Blackbeard had held to his course without waiting to fire that broadside, he would have cleared the end of the bar. Then he could have pointed back into the deeper water of the harbor. But now, with the sails flapping uselessly, and while Blackbeard shrieked profanity, his ship drifted with the current and edged slowly onto the beach. While he cursed, his men dumped everything movable over the side of the ship—everything movable, that is, except guns and ammunition. But the tide was running out by now, and the ship only wedged more firmly in the sand. There would be no

Everything movable was dumped overboard.

moving her until the tide rose again some six hours later.

And around the far end of the bar came Lieutenant Maynard and his sloop of war.

Blackbeard ordered his guns primed again. He held his order to fire until the last possible moment when Maynard's sloop seemed almost upon him. It was a blinding, smoking broadside, and the force of it made Maynard's helmsman sheer off. Peering through the clouds of smoke, Blackbeard gave a shout of triumph. On the deck of the sloop only two men were still on their feet—the helmsman and Maynard himself. As the sloop swung back toward the pirates, it looked as if she were out of control. Perhaps the broadside had disabled the rudder as well. It looked as if the rest would be easy.

At his prearranged signal, Blackbeard's men took up a new weapon which he had recently devised but had not yet tried out. It was a bottle filled with powder and shot. In each bottle was a slow-burning match. When Blackbeard gave the word, his men lit the matches. As the attacking ship swung into range, the bottles thumped onto her deck. Maynard and the helmsman had no chance to toss them into the water before most of them exploded. The air was filled with shrieking pieces of shot and broken glass. Maynard and the helmsman escaped being butchered by falling behind the companionway. They were barely on their feet again before Blackbeard's grappling irons had clamped across the bulwarks and twenty-three shouting, shooting pirates had thundered aboard the sloop.

It would have been quick, merciless slaughter, except for the fact that Maynard had two surprises for Blackbeard. The first was revealed immediately. The hatches opened and twenty-eight armed sailors swarmed onto the deck to meet the advancing pirates. Taken aback, the pirates halted for a moment and almost started to retreat. Blackbeard jumped into the rigging and, in an ear-splitting roar, promised his men worse treatment if they retreated than they would ever get if they advanced. They advanced. That was when they got their second surprise.

Blackbeard had taught his men well in deck fighting especially. He had no use for any weapon except the cutlass. The pistol in those days was nearly useless in hand-to-hand fighting because it fired only one shot. If a man paused to reload, he never got a chance to fire it again. The rapier was a long, thin shaft, lighter to use; and it would slip between a man's ribs or shoulder blades a lot more easily than the cutlass. But it was not always practical to dance about with a rapier on a crowded, blood-slicked deck.

Blackbeard preferred the heavy, broad-bladed cutlass. The cutlass had authority. When it connected at the end of a good swing, it could not fail. Even its flat side could bash in a man's head. A clean swipe which hit where it ought to, just at the Adam's apple, nearly always chopped off the man's head in one blow. This, Blackbeard taught his men, was the proper weapon for hand-to-hand combat on deck.

A secondary reason for using a cutlass was one which Blackbeard always kept in mind. The sight of the gory damage done by the cutlass usually took the fighting spirit out of anybody who tried to defend himself against the pirates' attack. So it was unnecessary to use the cutlass for long. But while they did, Blackbeard taught his men, they had to use it without pausing for a moment.

The principle of hand-to-hand fighting with the cutlass was one of constant motion. This was not the nimble dancing of the "fencing masters," as Blackbeard called the users of the rapier, but a slow, sure, steady onslaught. Day after day he made his men practice that attack, mainly to develop the necessary strength in the wrist.

A strong wrist was a necessity because the trick was to keep that big blade moving all the time, forehand and backhand, forehand and backhand. A good man with a cutlass did not stop to joust with anyone, Blackbeard always explained; he just kept moving. He trampled any bodies that got in the way, but he never stopped moving forward. If he stopped for a moment, he was a stationary target. So he kept

A heavy, broad-bladed cutlass was used by the pirates.

moving, and he kept that big blade moving, mowing down whatever came within range. He paid no attention to anything but the mass of enemies in front of him. He kept that big blade slicing until all had fallen. And until then, he never stopped that steady, slaughtering advance.

But Maynard's second surprise for Blackbeard was that he had figured out a possible way to beat the cutlass with the rapier.

Maynard knew as well as Blackbeard that a blood-covered deck was a dangerous place to dance about with a rapier. He knew that a man who slipped and fell near a cutlass-wielding pirate could have his head chopped off before he had a chance to get back into the fight. But Maynard had decided to use the rapier just the same, and he had armed his crew with rapiers.

This is why. Maynard realized that a cutlass weighed ten pounds. That is about the weight of five baseball bats. Imagine trying to swing five baseball bats with one hand, and you will begin to see what Maynard had in mind.

Probably Blackbeard never thought of this. Always before he and his men had made such a bloody slaughter with their cutlasses in a few minutes that their victims gave up. Blackbeard had never had to swing the big ten-pound cutlass for more than a few minutes at a time. That, at least, was what Maynard gambled on.

When you are playing chess or checkers, you

spend as much time thinking about the third
or fourth move as you do about the next one.
If you move this way, your opponent will probably move that way, and where will you be
then? This is how Maynard planned his big
battle with Blackbeard. He planned not so much
the opening minutes of the fight as the way it
would go half an hour later. And he planned
it so it *would* last half an hour or more. That is
why he chose rapiers. He had to prepare his
men to watch some of their shipmates butchered by those meat-cleaver cutlasses and not lose
their nerve. In the long run the pirates with
the heavy cutlasses would tire, and then the
sailors with their rapiers would pick them off.

So, as the pirates and the sailors of His Majesty's Navy came together, the attackers moved
in, cutting and slashing with their cutlasses.
All the while the defenders ducked and dodged,
flicking in and out with their thin, flashing
rapier blades. And the pirates began to win.

One by one the sailors fell before the scything
attack. The only defense was to bob and weave
and try to get in under the attacker's guard.

Every now and then a sailor did, slipping his long razor blade into a pirate. But mostly it was a devastating mass assault, with the pirates mowing the defenders down before them. It took only a couple of minutes for the numbers to become even as the sailors thumped to the deck, maimed or beheaded. Slashing and cutting his way through the surging mob, Blackbeard watched another sailor collapse and gave a bloodthirsty whoop. It would be over in a few minutes now.

But it was not over in a few minutes. Maynard had carefully trained his men for this first period of the battle. Again and again he had drilled into them the warning that they could expect no quarter from Blackbeard. Once the battle was joined, they had no choice but to keep on fighting to the death. If they tried to surrender, they would be cut to pieces. Their only hope for victory was to ignore the first wave of casualties, and to keep on parrying and thrusting. The longer the battle went on, the better their chances became.

Somehow enough of Maynard's sailors managed to keep on their feet and stay out of reach of those whirring cutlasses. And then the tide of battle began to turn.

There was no point at which it could have been said that the pirates started to lose and the sailors started to win. But the first definite signs came when the battle had been going on for more than half an hour. Here a pirate shifted his cutlass from one aching arm to the other and fell, with a neat hole pierced in his lungs by a rapier. There another pirate, wheezing with the effort, tried to rest his arm, then looked stupidly down at the cutlass on the deck and at the oozing stump which had been his hand before a rapier sliced off his fingers.

Over the rail lay another pirate, blubbering as the back of his ragged shirt reddened from half a dozen rapier thrusts. Across the rest of the deck other pirates grunted and swore and slipped and hacked away.

All the while the rapiers of His Majesty's Navy flicked in and out, in and out, pinking and stabbing and puncturing. And as the cutlass thrusts slowed, the rapiers flew even faster.

The sailors could smell victory now, and their blood was up. They moved from defense to attack, and kept it up. They did not slow the counterattack even when a lone pirate, with blood dripping onto the deck from a gashed thigh, bawled at the top of his lungs: *"Quarter!!"*

Probably Blackbeard did not even hear his man. He was battling two sailors at once. For the first time, he was fighting for his life. He had cut his way straight to the helm, where Maynard was waiting for him. A pirate tried to take a slice at Maynard, but Blackbeard grabbed his man and spun him across the deck, yelling, "Leave him alone! This one is mine!" Then, his great cutlass flashing in the morning sun, he waded in.

Maynard nimbly ducked the first attack, spinning away—but not quite quickly enough. The swishing cutlass caught the blade of Maynard's rapier, snapping it off neatly at the hilt.

Those were the days when, in a duel, a man who disarmed his opponent waited politely un-

til he could arm himself again. But this was no
duel. Blackbeard yelled with triumph and lum-
bered in for the kill.

Maynard did the only thing he could do at the
moment. He pitched the handle of his rapier
into Blackbeard's face. It caught him in the
mouth. Blackbeard shook his head, wiped the
blood into his beard and gave a hoarse laugh as
he came on.

But Maynard was not unarmed, as Blackbeard thought. He had one pistol left. He yanked
it free, aimed it at his attacker and fired.

The bullet struck Blackbeard in the left shoulder, too high. He barely slowed his advance,
ripping his shirt away from the wound as he
plunged on after his now helpless victim.

Maynard ducked under the attack, scrambled
across the deck to where a rapier lay in the
scuppers. But he slipped and sprawled on the
deck. He tried to get back on his feet, but he
was too late. Blackbeard was upon him.

And at this point Blackbeard made the mistake he had always warned his men against.

Never make yourself a stationary target, he

was forever telling them. Never stop moving
about. No matter how and where, keep moving.
But now the sight of a lieutenant in His Majesty's Royal Navy, lying in front of him cower-
ing, his arm held up in hopeless defense, was
too much for Blackbeard. He paused to enjoy
the moment before beheading the man.

And behind him a sailor hoisted a huge pike
in a backswing, its deadly two-edged blade glint-
ing as it moved. It came down in a full, whis-
tling arc, full force against the hulking, bearded
figure standing over the lieutenant.

This time Blackbeard staggered and howled
in agony. The heavy pike crunched into his col-
larbone between his right shoulder and ear. He
turned around to find his attacker, just as the
pike came crashing down again.

It caught him across the face, smashing his
nose and cutting open his forehead. The sailor
started to raise the pike a third time, but a
backhand slap of Blackbeard's cutlass sent him
skidding across the deck.

Maynard meanwhile scooped up the rapier
and attacked. The huge brute before him was

blinded by his own blood, staggering and spitting and cursing as he tried to see his attackers. Blood flowed from his gashed face and neck and from the pistol wound in his shoulder. But he roared for more fight.

Now all his enemies set upon him. He alone kept up the battle; all the other pirates had either been killed or disabled. One after another the sailors ducked in and thrust their rapier blades into him. From a safer distance others shot at him with their pistols. Others whacked at him with their pikes.

And still Blackbeard struck back. A bullet thudded into his buttocks. A pike caught him between the shoulder blades. Maynard sank his rapier in the broad belly. Blackbeard doubled up, but he would not go down.

Finally it had to be over. Blackbeard suddenly stiffened, swayed forward and crashed full length across the deck, like a falling tree. The ship trembled as he hit.

Maynard knelt over the mountainous hulk. There was no sign of life. It has been reported that Blackbeard had five bullets and twenty other wounds in him. Yet apparently he had actually died standing up.

Maynard rose and looked about the splintered, blood-washed deck. With the death of Blackbeard an eerie stillness had fallen on the scene. The only sound was an occasional groan from the crew, and the lap-lap of the rising water as the tide came in to free the stranded sloop. Maynard ordered his men—those who were still able to get about—to toss the great body over the side. But first they were to cut off the huge bearded head and hang it on the bowsprit. This would announce their victory when they returned home. This would tell everyone as they sailed up the James River that they had finally succeeded in killing the worst pirate of the Atlantic coast.

Maynard had more than three hours to wait for high tide when he could safely sail across the sand bar and out of the harbor. While he waited, he climbed aboard Blackbeard's ship and searched her hold. He was not surprised when he found no loot. Knowing he might be captured, Blackbeard had of course buried his treasure somewhere ashore. But Maynard *was* surprised when he found in Blackbeard's cabin some letters from Tobias Knight, the secretary of Governor Eden of North Carolina. The letters proved that the Governor and his secretary had helped Blackbeard sell his loot after his cruises.

These letters helped bring the Governor and his secretary to trial after Maynard had returned. But no such evidence was needed to try the pirates who had survived the battle. All except one, who proved he was not a pirate and had been forced into Blackbeard's crew, were found guilty. They were hanged.

There was one pirate who escaped the scaffold: Israel Hands, the same Israel Hands whom Blackbeard had shot as a crude practical joke the night before the battle. Hands had been taken ashore so a doctor could treat his shattered knee. So it was that Blackbeard saved his first mate's life. Israel Hands was ashore at the time of the last battle. Because of that he was the only pirate in Blackbeard's crew to escape the gallows.

4

Stede Bonnet, Gentleman Pirate

Stede Bonnet was the luckiest pirate who ever lived——while he lived.

More than 200 years ago, he was a wealthy plantation owner on the island of Barbados in the West Indies, but he gave it all up to go a-pirating. He had a fine mansion, acres of sugar cane, scores (perhaps more than a hundred) of slaves, a stable of excellent horses and the respect of everyone on the island. Yet he left it all behind to go sailing over the horizon as an outlaw.

He even paid for the building and outfitting of his pirate ship; he was probably the only pirate in history who did not steal his first ship. When he recruited his crew, he announced that he was planning to go trading among the islands. But he must have tipped off most of the men that they were in for a lot more adventure than a trading voyage, because apparently none of them deserted later when they found out what was really expected of them.

There were seventy of them, a huge crew for a trading ship. And any doubts they might have had were answered on the night when the ship rode the tide out of Barbados harbor. She carried ten guns. Her name, they discovered, was a favorite one for pirate ships—the *Revenge*. The year was 1717, the same year in which another pirate ship went sailing out of the harbor of New Providence, a few hundred miles to the north. That one was another *Revenge*. Her full name was *Queen Anne's Revenge*— Blackbeard's ship. Much like Blackbeard, Stede Bonnet was bound out on an adventure which would bring him a fortune he could never spend, fame he must have wished he had never earned, and death.

For Bonnet the fame and fortune came early. His new pirate ship had only been at sea a few days when the first victim was sighted. She was the *Anne,* from Glasgow, and she surrendered quickly. Stede Bonnet was a pirate; he was also a gentleman born and bred. The captain, crew and passengers of the *Anne* were courteously relieved of everything of value; and the *Anne* was sent on her way.

But although Bonnet was a gentleman with his victims, he was a martinet with his crew. A martinet is an extremely strict officer; the word comes from a Frenchman named Martinet, a seventeenth century drillmaster. That, or close to that, is what Bonnet himself had been. He was a former major in the British Army, and discipline in the British Army in those days was more than rugged; it was brutally cruel. Stede Bonnet was a prissy-looking man, short, fat and pompous in his waistcoat, breeches and knee buckles. That is probably why a few of the men in his crew made the mistake of thinking

that he would not assert his authority. They
found out otherwise quickly enough.

The first man to make an insulting remark
that was heard by the captain suddenly found
himself hung to the shrouds by the wrists.
While he swung back and forth with the motion of the ship, his feet just off the deck, his
shirt was ripped away and the knotted ropes of
the cat-o'-nine-tails laid onto his bare back.
His screams gradually faded as the whip beat
him into unconsciousness. Finally there was
nothing but the *swish-plop* of the "cat" and the
trickle of blood on the deck. Bonnet ordered
the man cut down and salt water splashed onto
his back. That brought him to, shrieking in
agony as he was hauled away and dumped in
his hammock. The rest of the crew, under Bonnet's orders, watched the performance. Anyone
else who was planning insubordination aboard
the *Revenge* changed his mind.

The whole crew, even including the man who
had served as an object lesson, was celebrating
the *Revenge*'s first capture when the second victim hove in sight. This one presented Stede

Bonnet ordered him hanged by the wrists and lashed.

Bonnet with a difficult dilemma. She was the *Turbet*. And she came from Barbados.

What should Bonnet do now? He had made a

point of telling everyone in Barbados that he was setting out on a trading voyage. Of course most of his island neighbors must have been suspicious—of the ten guns, the seventy crew members and the way Bonnet slipped out of the harbor in the dead of night. But no one could be sure. No one could be sure, that is, until someone reported that he had lost his ship to Bonnet.

And here was the *Turbet*, headed for her home port. If Bonnet captured her, robbed her and her crew and passengers and sent her on her way, the news would be all over Barbados as soon as she arrived. If Bonnet wanted to prevent this, he apparently had two alternatives: he could let the *Turbet* pass or he could take her and kill all aboard.

But Bonnet was both a pirate and a gentleman—too much a pirate to let the *Turbet* pass and too much of a gentleman to kill all aboard. He came up with a third alternative. He captured the *Turbet* and took everyone aboard as his prisoner. After all the cargo worth taking had been loaded aboard the *Revenge*, the *Turbet*'s people watched their ship burn to the water's edge and sink. Then, a few weeks later, they were put ashore on another island, far off the regular shipping lanes through the West Indies. It would be many months before they could reach Barbados with the news that Stede Bonnet had indeed turned pirate.

Why did Bonnet do this? Why did he worry about what they thought of him back home? Did he think that he might someday want to return and settle down again as a respectable plantation owner? Did he really believe that he could go gallivanting around as a pirate and then come home and not pay for it? We shall see.

Bonnet's astonishing good luck continued. The loot from the *Anne* and the *Turbet* was pushed aside in the hold to make way for more plunder, from two more ships, the *Endeavor* and the *Young*. So fast did the treasure pile up that Bonnet had to find a place to get rid of it. He sailed up the North Atlantic coast, all the way to Long Island Sound. There he put into the harbor of Gardiners Island.

This was a favorite pirate hide-out of the time. Some merchants did not care where they bought their goods so long as they got a bargain. So they would come out to the tip of Long Island, sail across to Gardiners Island and buy the loot from pirates. Like all stolen merchandise, pirate loot was sold for about a quarter of its actual value. But when it had been taken into New York City, the merchant could sell it just below normal prices and make a nice profit. So the business flourished. Bonnet was one of thousands who got rid of their plunder this way.

With silver dollars bulging their pockets and sea bags, Bonnet's men could hardly wait to sail down to New Providence, the town which probably had more taverns and gambling houses than any other in the New World. The *Revenge* was speeding full sail down the coast toward New Providence when she crossed the path of a big East Indiaman, armed with forty guns. Bonnet was at the point of putting the helm hard over and getting out of there as fast as he could. Just then the big ship broke out her flag, the skull and crossbones. Vastly relieved, Bonnet decided to join forces with the other pirate. That, of course, was where he made his mistake, for the pirate was Blackbeard.

You have read about the rich cruise Blackbeard went on, with Bonnet as his unwilling guest. But despite the fact that fortune still favored him and prizes appeared periodically, Bonnet began to take an intense dislike to piracy. The sight of Blackbeard, with his greasy, matted beard, the bulging, bloodshot eyes, the torn, begrimed clothes and the huge, slobbering mouth was enough to cure anyone. Bonnet was heard by his crew to mutter that if he ever got out of Blackbeard's grip, he would give it all up. He would go back to Barbados and never have anything to do with piracy again—that is, if he ever could return to Barbados. For that matter, he doubted that he could ever look an honest Englishman in the face again. One thing he knew: he was through with piracy.

As soon as Blackbeard turned him loose, Bonnet lived up to his word. Once aboard his ship, he steered a course straight for Bath Town.

There, with Blackbeard, he met the Governor of North Carolina, Charles Eden. Then he discovered that Eden had made a handy little business of dealing with pirates. Bonnet thought that he and Eden could come to terms.

From one of Blackbeard's victims, Bonnet had learned that England's King George III had declared an "amnesty." That meant that any pirate who would give himself up and pledge never to return to piracy again could be pardoned and escape all punishment. This seems an impractical way to fight piracy, but actually it worked pretty well. There simply were too many pirates for the British Navy to chase down and put out of business. And Parliament would not increase funds for the Navy, just to go pirate hunting.

But while there were too many pirates for the Navy, there were also beginning to be too many pirates for the pirates. That is, the competition was getting tough. Because the Atlantic, and especially the Caribbean, literally swarmed with pirates, merchant captains were sailing in convoys. Gold, silver, coins and jewels were no longer being carried by lone, lightly armed ships. For every ship with a cargo worth plundering there were half a dozen pirate ships out looking for her. So the pickings were getting slim.

The success of Bonnet's and Blackbeard's cruises at this time showed they had amazing luck. More important, it showed they both had some kind of sixth sense for sniffing out the areas where well-stocked merchantmen happened to be. It was because of the slim pickings for pirates of the time that His Majesty's Government came up with the idea of pardoning any who would give themselves up.

Once you are an outlaw, you generally remain one. Though you may wish you hadn't become one, it is too late. To quit, you must pay for your crimes. But here was a chance to wipe the slate clean. Here was a chance to go straight with no penalties for past "mistakes." The plan worked quite well. Hundreds of pirates surrendered their ships—with the loot they had been unable to bury somewhere—and were granted pardons so they could return to legitimate employment.

Then the plan began to backfire. Blackbeard was one of the first to discover how useful a pardon was in his operations. When pursuit got too hot, when merchant ships seemed to disappear from the seas for a while, or simply when he wanted a bit of a rest, all he had to do was to give himself up. With the help of Governor Eden, Blackbeard received an official pardon and could relax until he felt like going a-pirating again. More and more pirates like Blackbeard used the "King's Amnesty" as a convenient device for time out between plundering cruises.

Not Bonnet. To him the amnesty was a godsend. He sailed into Bath Town, surrendered his ship, crew, loot and himself, and received his pardon from Governor Eden. This was what he had promised himself during all those long weeks when he had been a prisoner aboard Blackbeard's ship. He had had enough of piracy, and he could not dream of a better way to quit.

He had had his crazy adventure, and now he did not have to pay the penalty. He could return to Barbados a free man, and settle down to an easy life again on his plantation.

But he didn't. Within a few weeks from the time when he received his pardon, Stede Bonnet was at sea again, in his same ship. Her name was changed to the *Royal James*. His was changed from Bonnet to Thomas. But the ship carried the black flag of the pirate.

Why? More than 200 years of research has produced only two possible answers to the mystery. One is that Bonnet had heard that Blackbeard was on the loose again, which he was. Bonnet still smarted under the shame of being Blackbeard's prisoner. Bonnet was no coward, and he wanted revenge. Perhaps he went back to sea mainly to run down Blackbeard and settle accounts with him. Perhaps, but no one really knows.

The other possible reason is that when Bonnet thought seriously about returning home to Barbados, he could not bring himself to do it. Even though he had his pardon, he could no

longer be the respectable leader of the community as he had been before. Always he would
be pointed out as the man who had been a
bloody pirate. But worse than his neighbors' reaction was that of Mrs. Bonnet. She was famous
as a terrible nag. The more Bonnet thought of
returning to Barbados, to his disapproving
neighbors—and to Mrs. Bonnet—the more he
came around to the idea that being a pirate was
not so bad after all.

And so he went back a-pirating.

Now he discovered how few richly laden ships
there really were in the Atlantic. As Captain
Thomas of the *Royal James,* he took twelve
ships in fast order. But he got little valuable
plunder for his efforts. The first carried provi-
sions, the next some rum, the next two tobacco,
the next pork and bacon, the next combs, pins
and needles, the next leather hides, followed by
a sloop with a miscellaneous cargo, another with
foodstuffs, another with molasses and rum and
about twenty-five pounds in cash. Only one of
the entire dozen carried any money in coins.

By this time the hull of the *Royal James* had

become encrusted with barnacles, festooned with seaweed and riddled by teredo, the worm that eats into wooden hulls in warm southern waters.

Bonnet had kept two of the ships he had captured, and with them he had made up a little fleet. Now he sailed down around Cape Fear, on the coast of North Carolina, and turned up the river. Nearly a mile up the Cape Fear River he ran the *Royal James* onto the shore and waited for the tide to run out. When the ship was nearly high and dry, he had lines made fast to her masts and run to pulleys in the trees ashore. The crew went to work hauling on the ropes, and slowly the *Royal James* creaked over on her side so repairs could be made to her hull.

When he could get a good look at the ship's bottom, Bonnet could see that whole new timbers would be needed for repairs. As he wondered how he could get them, his lookouts reported that a small vessel had put into the river and anchored, down around the bend. As soon as it was dark, Bonnet sent his boats down river.

Slipping under the stern of the visitor, the pirates climbed aboard and captured her. At the next high tide the prize was sailed alongside the *Royal James* and sent ashore. The needed timbers were chopped out of her.

But here Bonnet made a tactical error. Since he wanted only the ship, he put the captain and crew ashore on the beach before she was torn apart. Apparently some of the survivors made their way to Charles Town. There the news quickly spread—a pirate named Thomas, who had captured a great number of ships and had two with him as prizes, was holed up in the Cape Fear River making repairs to his flagship. At that point a strange kind of pirate hunter stepped forward to offer to chase down "Captain Thomas."

This pirate hunter was not a naval officer but a colonel in the British Army. His name was William Rhett. Colonel Rhett went to South Carolina's Governor Robert Johnson requesting permission to outfit two ships and go in search of the pirate. He had no trouble getting the permission, and he made his preparations quickly. Only a few days after he had volunteered, Rhett's two ships, carrying 130 officers and men, sailed out of Charles Town Harbor.

They reached Cape Fear on the evening of September 26, 1718. As they sailed into the mouth of the river, Colonel Rhett could see the masts of the three ships in behind the sand dunes. He had caught them in the trap.

His quarry did not realize this for a short while. Bonnet saw the masts of the two sloops slide into the river and promptly sent his boats down, after dark, for another capture. His men returned with the news: the visitors had run aground with the falling tide. But they were still in the river, waiting for the next rising water. Both ships were heavily armed sloops of war.

Bonnet had one consolation. He knew that he could take all night to get ready. With the tide still falling, his pursuer would not try to come up the river even if he could work his sloops free. Bonnet used the time well. All night he and his men made their preparations. The water tubs and blankets were put near the powder magazine. The light sails were sent down, and the other sails were soaked in alum so they would not catch fire so easily. Shrouds were doubled or replaced with chain, so they could not be shot away. Nets were hung along the rail to hold back the boarding parties. Cannon were run out, and their carriages were greased. Heavy restraining ropes were fastened to them, because a ship's cannon kicked so violently in those days that it sometimes bounced against the beams of the deck overhead.

While his men made ready, Bonnet figured out his strategy. He decided not to wait like a rat in the trap. He would make a run for it, with the first light of dawn.

There were a number of ways he could do this. He could send one of his prizes down, as a feint. While the pursuers went after that ship, he could sail past them and out into the open water in the *Royal James,* which was now fully repaired. This could have been a successful trick in wider waters. But it was a doubtful maneuver in the narrow channel of the Cape Fear River. If his decoy ship went far enough off on either side of the river channel to lure the pursuers out of range of the *Royal James,* the decoy probably would go aground.

Another device might have been a mass attack on the two sloops of war by the three ships of Bonnet's fleet. But while he would outnumber his pursuers, he probably would not outgun them. He would have to spread his artillery thin in order to take all three of his ships into the battle. And again, the twisting channels of the Cape Fear River were no place for the maneuvers necessary for a five-ship battle.

So Bonnet decided to risk all in his one ship, the reconditioned *Royal James.* Perhaps, as indicated by their running aground, the pursuers did not know the channels of the river very well. Using his knowledge of the channels and the shoals, Bonnet might be able to lead them aground again. If not, the surprise and the sheer weight of his massed strength in one ship should make it possible for him to blast his way through to the open Atlantic and out of the trap.

Gray dawn was creeping across the sky before all was ready aboard the *Royal James.* There

would be no time for sleep, even if anyone
could have slept. Bonnet waited only until the
first daylight breezes hummed in the rigging of
the *Royal James*. Then he gave the command.

With anchor dripping at her bow and the
water rippling under her, the ship gathered
speed as she headed down river. Her men assembled at their battle stations. The matches were
lit at the guns. Everyone watched the bend in
the river and the masts of the two sloops of war.

The morning breeze was growing and so was
the current as the tide moved down the river
and out into the sea. At the mouth of the Cape
Fear River there is a wide bay, sweeping around
to the narrow entrance. This makes the tide
race through the entrance, and Bonnet was
counting on that to take him on past the sloops
even if the wind failed.

Maybe Colonel Rhett realized this, maybe
not. But in any case, he had figured out his
strategy too. He did not intend to engage in the
normal broadsides of sea warfare, the side-to-
side blasting away which was the custom of His
Majesty's Navy. He did not know whether Bon-

net intended to make a run for it. But he figured that if Bonnet did, his only hope lay in racing past the two sloops, firing his broadsides as he went. So Rhett decided to avoid that kind of battle. Instead of employing the usual tactics of the pirate chaser, he would try the usual tactics of the pirate.

. Bonnet found this out as soon as he got within range. At his first broadside he expected the sloops to come alongside and fire away. But they did not. To his surprise, they kept right on course toward him. And as they came, he could see the grappling hooks hung on the bulwarks. Obviously the sloops were coming in to grapple the *Royal James* and board.

Bonnet took a long chance. In a way, he had no choice. He could not afford to get tangled up with his pursuers because his entire strategy depended upon his ability to keep moving on down the river toward the sea. They could fire at him, sweep his deck, even cut up his rigging. But so long as he could keep moving, he stood a good chance of getting away. If they once got those grappling hooks over his bulwarks, though, they had him.

So Bonnet turned and ran for the shallows. He well knew that he was taking the risk of running aground. But he hoped to entice his pursuers onto the shoals too. Then he would slip back into the channel and leave them floundering on one of the sand bars. Gradually the *Royal James* started edging into the shoal water, followed by the sloops of war.

The plan worked. One of the sloops suddenly came to a halt, hard aground. Her men had barely started shouting when the other sloop grounded too. Bonnet must have smiled as he ordered the helm over so as to duck back into the deeper water.

But he was too late. With a sickening lurch the *Royal James* rode up onto a sand bar and stuck fast.

So the battle, far from being over, had started in earnest. One of the sloops of war was just within range of the *Royal James* as the canonading started. What followed was one of the strangest sea battles ever fought—between two army officers, aboard ships which lay over on their sides in the mud.

The broadsides were ineffective because of the lean of the ships. Not only could the vessels not maneuver during the battle, but they could not even bring their guns to bear. Here Bonnet's luck was still with him. As the tide ran out under Colonel Rhett's sloop, she rolled over so that the guns on the side toward Bonnet pointed down into the mud. Bonnet's ship rolled the other way. Try as they could, Bonnet's men could not wedge the guns down so as to fire on the sloop's deck. But Bonnet was able to fire into her rigging at will. This he did while his men covered the sloop's deck with small arms fire.

Colonel Rhett tried to place his men in positions on deck where they could return the fire. But with the sloop tipped over so that the entire deck was exposed, and with Bonnet's ship leaning away so that her bulwarks protected the pirates, there was little Rhett could do. It was an uneven battle, and it lasted five hours. In the meantime, Bonnet's guns cut the sloop's rigging into a tangle, and his small arms fire killed ten of Rhett's men and wounded fourteen. Meanwhile the other sloop lay out of range. It seemed only a matter of time before the tide would rise, freeing the *Royal James* and letting her escape down the river while Rhett watched in exasperation from his crippled sloop.

That was when Stede Bonnet's luck finally deserted him. Although he could not have known it, the *Royal James* was on slightly higher ground than Rhett's sloops. As the tide crept in, the first to float was the sloop with Rhett aboard. He took her into deeper water, out of range of Bonnet's guns, and made some hasty repairs to the shot-up rigging. Then, while Bonnet waited in frustrated fury and the *Royal James* still heeled over in the shallow water, Rhett's second sloop swung free. It was nearly half an hour before Bonnet's ship began to creak onto an even keel. By that time both of Rhett's sloops had worked down between him and the river entrance. Now they closed in for the kill.

But there was no more battle. The white flag of surrender fluttered to the masthead of the

Royal James. Rhett made a cautious approach—wisely, it turned out. Bonnet had planned to blow up the *Royal James* and her pursuers as soon as they came alongside. But some members of the crew, no doubt figuring that they could save their lives and also escape the hangman because of their act, had at last mutinied and overpowered their tyrannical captain. So Rhett was ferried across to the *Royal James.* There, to his surprise, he found for the first time that he had captured not an obscure "Captain Thomas" but the famous Stede Bonnet himself.

The city of Charles Town had no formal jail, so Stede Bonnet's pirates were locked up in a watchhouse when they were brought in. Bonnet and his sailing master, David Herriot, were put in the custody of the city marshal. While a full company of militia guarded the crew, only two guards stood watch outside the house where Bonnet and his sailing master were kept.

This arrangement lasted for nineteen days while the authorities prepared for the trial of

As the white flag went up, Rhett ferried across.

the pirates. Then, just before their trial was to start, Bonnet and Herriot disappeared.

Again Colonel Rhett went after them. A report of a stolen boat suggested that the two fugitives had tried to slip out of the harbor. Since the boat seemed too small for the open Atlantic, Rhett guessed that his quarry had gone to one of the islands in the harbor. He started a systematic search of them all.

His guess was partly wrong. Bonnet had sailed straight out into the open ocean. But his famous luck had apparently deserted him for good. The weather got so bad that he and Herriot had to put back into the harbor. They went ashore on Sullivan's Island, near the harbor entrance, to lie low until the bad weather blew over.

The bad weather held for a week. Meanwhile someone on Sullivan's Island spotted the two suspicious-looking men and reported them to the Charles Town authorities. On the night of November fifth, Rhett and his searching party crept up on Bonnet's camp. Without warning they emptied their pistols into the group around the fire, killing Herriot and wounding an Indian and Negro who had joined them. Bonnet was not wounded, but this time he was placed under heavy guard.

On Monday, November 10, 1718, two days after his crewmen had been hanged in a group, Bonnet went on trial. He was quickly found guilty. Sir Nicholas Trot, Judge of the Vice-Admiralty and Chief Justice of the Province of South Carolina, looked down at the ragged but aristocratic figure before him. Aloud he wondered how a respectable, wealthy former officer of His Majesty's Army had come to this. But whatever Bonnet's motives had been, he had taken innumerable vessels, including a dozen since receiving the King's Pardon. The judge had no choice; he had to exact the penalty.

"I must now," Sir Nicholas intoned, "do my office as judge. The sentence that the law hath appointed to pass upon you for your offenses, and which this court doth therefore award, is that you, the said Stede Bonnet, shall go from hence to the place from whence you came, and from thence to the place of execution, where you shall be hanged by the neck until you are dead.

"And the God of infinite mercy be merciful to your soul."

Marching behind a silver-painted oar, the traditional symbol of punishment for piracy, Stede Bonnet went to the gallows on White Point in Charles Town. The noose was put around his neck. A bunch of wild flowers, another pirate tradition, was stuck into his bound hands. At the signal, the floor fell from beneath him. He died so quietly that the flowers did not even fall from his hands.

5

Pirate Oddities

Nearly all the pirates of the New World were oddities in their own oddly assorted ways. Stede Bonnet, the wealthy army major turned pirate captain, was one. But there were many more. For example take Pierre le Grand, who is sometimes called the father of piracy in the West Indies. Pierre le Grand set up his base of operations on Tortuga Island, off the coast of what is now Haiti. He did not have much luck at first. But then he planned and carried out one of the boldest attacks in the history of piracy, or in all maritime history, for that matter. When word of his exploit got around, hundreds of adventurers tried to imitate it. Practically none succeeded.

Pierre le Grand succeeded because to fail meant death for himself and his entire crew. He was watching from his island hide-out one day in the mid-seventeenth century when he saw a huge Spanish fleet sail past. One galleon, larger than all the rest, was lagging behind. Pierre le Grand and his men decided to try to take her in an open boat.

As dusk came and darkness swiftly lowered on the sea, the little boat put out toward the becalmed galleon. And while some of the pirates pulled at the oars, others bored small holes in the bottom of the boat. It was left to sink behind them when they climbed aboard the galleon. And so they had no choice but to fight, to victory or to the death.

The galleon's towering stern lanterns glowed above them. Still no cry came from the lookout. The pirates, each armed with a pistol and sword, caught hold of the chain plates and slithered quickly up the galleon's sides. The lookout was asleep. He never woke again. The helmsman was killed before he had a chance to cry the alarm.

While the other pirates disarmed the crew, Pierre le Grand and a few men surprised the admiral in his cabin. The admiral was playing cards with his officers. Le Grand took them prisoner. Those aboard who had not tried to resist, and thus were still alive, were herded together with the officers. The galleon was sailed over near the shore, and all were set on the beach.

Now Pierre le Grand and his men had a huge warship with which they could devastate shipping all over the world. What did they do? They divided the store of silver in the galleon's great hold. Then they sailed the galleon across the Atlantic to France and took her into an out-of-the-way port. They left her there, spreading ashore, dispersing and settling down with their plunder. Pierre le Grand had made his fortune in one venture. He lived to a ripe old age, but he never went a-pirating again.

Another pirate with a short, successful career —a real pioneer in the profession—was Dixey Bull. He is generally regarded as the first pirate in New England waters. Dixey Bull came from a prominent London family and through them received from the king a grant of land at York, in what is now the state of Maine. He moved there in 1631, and settled down to a respectable life as a trader.

But in June of 1632 a French ship came into Penobscot Bay and seized Bull's little craft, with its cargo of "coats, ruggs, blanketts, bisketts, etc." Either because he was maddened by this attack or because it made him realize how easy it was to plunder, Bull turned pirate.

For a year he terrorized the New England coast, capturing dozens of vessels. Finally the authorities in Boston sent out armed sloops to take him. They never found him. No one knows for sure, but Dixey Bull apparently sailed

Quickly the pirates slithered up the galleon's sides.

home to England to settle down, as Pierre le
Grand had done, in a pleasant retirement enjoying his easily-won loot.

It might almost be argued that Dixey Bull
was forced into piracy. But there were many
pirates who were forced a great deal more than
Dixey Bull was; they were captured and given
no other choice. One example among thousands
was John Fillmore, a fisherman from Ipswich,
Massachusetts. John Fillmore was minding his
own business, fishing for cod on the Grand
Banks, off the New England coast. A pirate
named Captain Phillips spotted the little fishing
vessel and captured it without a shot.

The fishermen were ordered to become pirates or be killed then and there. They decided
to become pirates. But they waited for their
chance. A few days later they mutinied and took
the ship away from the pirates. They brought
the pirate ship into Boston harbor, turned it
and the pirates over to the authorities and went
proudly home. John Fillmore then would have
disappeared from history—except for the fact

that he was the only pirate who was also an ancestor of a President of the United States. Millard Fillmore was his great-grandson.

Charles Gibbs is another pirate who would argue that he had been forced into becoming one, but it would only have been true of the second time he became one. Born in Rhode Island in 1794, Gibbs was first a seaman in the U.S. Navy. He served with distinction aboard the *Chesapeake* in her famous battle against the British frigate *Shannon* in the War of 1812. The *Chesapeake* lost that battle, despite the famous battle cry of her commander: "Don't give up the ship." Gibbs went to the infamous Dartmoor Prison in England. Shortly after the war ended, he was on the high seas as a pirate, using a hide-out in Cuba as a base and capturing ships all through the Caribbean. By 1819 he had made a fortune of about $30,000 in gold. Apparently no one could prove anything against him, because he was living comfortably in New York City. A few years later, however, he took a pleasure trip to Liverpool, and here fate repaid him. On the high seas he was ensnared by a lady thief, who got away with most of the fortune he had won as a pirate. Obviously Gibbs had no choice; he became a pirate again.

He did only fairly well this time. After a year he was caught. He was hanged in New York City in 1831.

Then there was a Captain Kennedy (no one knows his first name) who was a kind of latter-day pirate. Captain Kennedy sailed as a pirate, took ships as a pirate and apparently even buried treasure as a pirate. But he always preferred and continued to practice his first profession: he was a pickpocket.

Even when the luckless crew of some victim had been hauled aboard the pirate ship and separated from everything of value, Captain Kennedy could not resist sidling up to one of the men and slipping a hand into his empty pocket, just to keep in practice.

Kennedy was no navigator. When he and his crew tried to sail their ship, the *Rover*, to

Ireland, they missed the country entirely and wound up off the coast of Scotland. They ran the ship ashore and let the sea break her up. Kennedy got to Dublin, where he spent all his money, and then went across to Deptford, England. There he was arrested for picking pockets again, among other things. Since the other things included highway robbery and piracy, Captain Kennedy was hanged on the gallows at Execution Dock.

The case of John Upton was not so easy to decide. John Upton had lived an honest life until July of 1723, when his wife died. Upton found that she had left him so many debts that he was in danger of being arrested by his creditors. Since those were the days of debtors' prisons, Upton had to flee before the police caught up with him. He found a berth as a boatswain aboard a ship bound for Newfoundland.

Two years later he was serving aboard another ship, running between Barbados and Bristol, when she was taken by a pirate. Whether Upton was forced or not, he became a member of the pirate crew. He escaped shortly thereafter, getting ashore on the Central American coast, where the Spaniards arrested him as a spy.

After a few months in prison he was put aboard a ship in Porto Bello to be sent to Spain. Somehow he escaped the prison ship and got to another ship which took him to Jamaica. He arrived there in time to be caught by one of the "press gangs." These were the bands of men who rounded up everyone they could lay hands on and forced them aboard British men-of-war. Upton was dragged aboard H.M.S. *Nottingham*, where he served for two years.

Then suddenly the charge of piracy was brought against him. He was put in irons and shipped to London. In the trial he maintained that he was innocent. He had a journal which he claimed to have carried with him ever since shipping out as a boatswain; in the journal he had written that he had been forced to become a pirate. But witnesses were presented who swore that Upton had willingly become a pirate and, in fact, was one of the cruelest of them all. He was found guilty and sentenced to hang.

Six years earlier Upton had left four children behind when he went to sea. He did not have a chance to see them before he was hanged.

A more fortunate pirate than Upton, for a while anyway, was Thomas Veale. With three of his shipmates Veale came ashore in Massachusetts in the middle of the seventeenth century. Apparently they had had a successful career as pirates and were retiring from the sea. Three of them retired whether they had planned to or not, it turned out. They were captured, sent to England, tried and hanged.

Thomas Veale escaped. He lived in Massachusetts for some years afterward, working as a shoemaker and making periodic visits to a mysterious cave in the Lynn Woods. It was said that he had stored his share of the pirate treasure in this cave. If this were so, no one could figure out why he worked as a shoemaker. No one could figure out, either, why he never spent any of the treasure in the town. But he kept making his trips to the cave. And no one else dared enter the dark and ghostly hole. Then, in 1658, there was a severe earthquake in New England. Thomas Veale was in his "treasure cave." The cave opening was covered over by a landslide of rocks. No one bothered to try to dig him out.

Fully as odd as the miser Thomas Veale was the pirate-churchman Captain Daniel. His first name, like that of many pirates, has been lost and forgotten. But his actions will long be remembered. One of the bloodiest pirates, Captain Daniel was also one of the most religious.

The best-remembered occasion in his career occurred when he anchored off a small island near Dominica, one of the Windward Islands of the West Indies. Daniel sent some men ashore to capture a priest. As soon as the terrified man of God had been dragged aboard, Daniel ordered everyone down on his knees for Mass. The ceremony started with a broadside of artillery that made the deck shake under them.

The priest was part way through his fervent prayers when Daniel shouted at one of the crew to stop muttering. The crewman answered Daniel back. Daniel whipped out his pistol and shot the man through the head. As he blew the smoke from the barrel, he asked if anyone else wished to show disrespect for the Mass. To the trembling priest Daniel said, "Do not be troubled, father. He is a rascal lacking in his duty, and I have punished him to teach him better." A bystander who later recounted the incident remarked that this was an effective way to make sure that disrespect for the Mass would not be repeated—at least by that particular pirate.

Another pirate who combined piracy with Christian charity was Captain Greaves. His first name has been forgotten because no one ever called him anything but Red Legs Greaves. He was the son of a Scottish family sent from England to Barbados as slaves by Oliver Cromwell during the Civil War in England. Because the Scottish and Irish slaves in the West Indies continued to go about bare-kneed, they came to be called "red legs."

As a pirate Red Legs Greaves captured a great

many ships. But he never killed or tortured a prisoner. He wounded no more than was necessary in order to take a ship. In fact, he became a pirate captain after a disagreement with his commander over the torture of a prisoner. The disagreement was settled in a duel, which Greaves won. After he was elected captain, he refused even to let his men rob the seamen of a captured ship.

After his greatest victory, the taking of a small Spanish fleet, Greaves retired to the West Indies island of Nevis, where he became a wealthy planter. One day a seaman preferred charges against him as a pirate. Greaves was imprisoned in a dungeon to await trial. That was in 1680, and in that year came an earthquake which destroyed the dungeon. Tidal waves flooded the entire town, and Greaves was one of the few survivors.

He escaped by shipping aboard a whaler and later returned to Nevis. He was finally pardoned —in return for his help in capturing a band of pirates. Retiring again as a plantation owner, Greaves prospered, donating most of his fortune to charity. At his death he was mourned by the entire population of the island.

There were other "kindly" pirates. Probably the kindliest was one Captain Misson, a Frenchman who was being brought up to be an army officer by his father, until the young student decided that he would rather go to sea. He was training in navigation at Naples when he made a holiday trip to Rome. There he met Signor Carracioli. The Signor was not only responsible for Misson's turning pirate, but he was also responsible for the crew they got together becoming the strangest band of pirates who ever tossed a grappling hook.

In a ship provided by Misson and named the *Victoire*, they sailed for the West Indies. There they fought and captured an English man-of-war, the *Winchester*, off Martinique. At Carracioli's urging they flew not the usual black flag of piracy but a white one embroidered with the motto, "For God and Liberty." Their aim would be to take only what they needed and to take it only from those who could well afford it. A hold full of ill-gotten plunder, they swore, was the last thing in the world they wanted.

Somehow along the way this original goal changed. The *Victoire's* hold did fill with plunder. But Misson, Carracioli and company always took it from their victims in the pleasantest manner possible. The first ship they captured was an English sloop under the command of a Captain Thomas Butler. They relieved the sloop of a few barrels of rum and some other necessities. In the process they treated Captain Butler and his men so well that when the pirates returned to the *Victoire* they were sent on their way with three rousing cheers.

The *Victoire* then crossed the Atlantic to the coast of Africa. There the pirates captured a Dutch ship loaded with slaves. Promptly the slaves were freed. After watching the pirates in action, and no doubt comparing their behavior with that of their own captain, many of the sailors from the slave ship deserted to join the pirate crew. Misson welcomed them—until a few days later when he caught one of them swearing.

How it was possible for a few minutes to go by without a sailor swearing loud enough to be heard throughout the ship in those days is a mystery. Perhaps Captain Misson preferred not to hear it until it became unbearable. In any case, he immediately ordered all hands to the quarterdeck, where he delivered a little lecture. It was an extraordinary lecture to be delivered on the deck of a pirate ship.

Misson began by explaining that before the Dutchmen had joined the crew he had never allowed "the name of the great Creator profaned" aboard the *Victoire*. Now he found that the Dutchmen were cursing and even that some of his own men had taken it up. Such vices as this, he said, were what "degenerated men into brutes, by drowning that only faculty which distinguishes between man and beast, reason." He warned the crew that he "could not see them run into these odious vices without a sincere concern," since he had a fatherly affection for them. He would be ashamed of himself, he said, for being "neglectful of the common good" if he did not "admonish them." Then he told them what the admonishment would be.

The first man caught swearing aboard the *Victoire* would be brought to the shrouds, hung there by his thumbs and lashed on the bare back until it was a pulp. Then he would be doused with buckets of salt water. Misson went on to say that he was sure that on reflection everyone would agree that there was little pleasure to be had from such a vice as swearing. He was sure his men would get the idea. His men thought of the lash and the bucket of salt water and got the idea.

Luck followed Misson and his "Christian pirates." Everywhere ships surrendered to them. Every captain expressed his surprise at the decency with which he and crew and passengers were treated. Then, during a battle with a British ship, the English captain was killed. Misson was overwhelmed with grief. At his orders a solemn burial service was held on a nearby beach. One of the pirates, who had formerly been a stonecutter, made an impressive headstone engraved with the words, "Here lies a gallant English Man." Misson ordered a volley of fifty guns

A solemn funeral was held for the English captain.

fired over the grave. Then the pirates sailed away with £60,000 they had taken from the Englishmen.

When Misson and his men had finally tired of this kind of carrying on, they sailed for the island of Madagascar, the great pirate capital of the world. There they set up a small socialistic state called Libertatia. It had no private ownership and no free enterprise. When the economy of their state began to run down, Misson and

Carracioli simply armed another ship, went out a-pirating again and returned to refill the treasury. For some years Libertatia lasted this way until the surrounding natives, apparently feeling crowded, gathered a large force and drove the settlers into the sea. Misson and a few others managed to get away without being killed. But their ship was driven ashore by a hurricane. All hands, including Captain Misson, were drowned.

There are some similarities between the Frenchman Captain Misson and Captain Cobham, who came from Dorsetshire, England. Like Misson, Cobham was extremely lucky as a pirate. Like Misson, Cobham spent most of his life under the influence of a companion of far stronger will than his. But here the similarity ends. While Captain Misson's companion was a kindhearted signor, Captain Cobham's companion was a veritable devil of a woman, who was also his wife.

Apparently Cobham was an insignificant smuggler who had only recently turned pirate when he called at Plymouth, England, and met Maria. Her influence appears in the way Cobham started treating his prisoners after she moved aboard the pirate ship. He had not tried to act like a Misson, exactly. In fact, he had sunk his last prize, letting the captain and crew go down with her. Now he began to show not just cruelty but fiendish imagination as well.

Crossing the Atlantic, Cobham prowled the coast of Nova Scotia and New England, capturing and sinking several ships. But instead of letting the crew go down with the ship, he and Maria employed more interesting ways for them to die. The members of one crew were tied in sacks and dumped overboard. On another ship the pirates held the captain while Maria tried out a little dagger she had recently stolen, to see if it really would kill. It did. On another ship Maria tested a new pistol. The captain and two mates were tied to the windlass of their ship for her target practice. This kind of killing began to bore her, though, and she tried a few experiments with poison, using various amounts of it on her victims and noting how lingering and painful their deaths were.

Perhaps because of the sight of Maria, in her favorite naval uniform, shooting, stabbing and poisoning, Captain Cobham decided that he had had enough. But Maria had not. She talked him into keeping at sea until finally they had collected so much loot that they had to get rid of some of it. Besides, their crew was on the verge of mutiny.

Cobham finally persuaded Maria to quit the sea by promising her a mansion on the French coast. The estate he bought had a little harbor of its own, in which they kept a pleasure yacht. And so they gave up piracy—almost.

On a pleasant day when they were sailing across the harbor for a picnic, they decided to pay a social visit to a big West Indiaman which lay at anchor just outside the bay. They were received hospitably and were enjoying the visit when suddenly the temptation became overpowering. No more than a signal of agreement was needed between the couple. Cobham whipped out a pistol and shot his host through the head. Maria meanwhile called the yacht's crew aboard.

With their help she rounded up and killed the crew of the merchantman. Cobham and his wife sailed their prize to Bordeaux, where they were able to sell her with no questions asked. They returned to the estate, their yacht, to peace and quiet, and to their memories.

And, perhaps, to their consciences, because only a few weeks later Maria died of poison. Did she kill herself? Or did her husband finally become so disgusted with the fiend he had married that he poisoned her himself? No one knows.

Whatever the cause of Maria's death, her husband never paid the price of piracy. Not only that, he lived out his remaining years in wealthy respectability. When he died, he was one of the best-loved members of the community.

The end did not come so happily for a pirate named Charles Bellamy. After a start as a "wrecker," one who salvaged (and sometimes caused) shipwrecks, in the West Indies, Bellamy launched himself as a pirate along the coast of New England. He did extremely well, and he might have been able to retire some day as a successful pirate had it not been for what happened off Cape Cod one night in 1726.

At that time Bellamy had a whole fleet of pirate vessels. He was en route from Placentia Bay in Newfoundland, to Nantucket Island, off the south coast of Massachusetts. There he spied, chased and captured a small whaleship named the *Mary Anne*.

Legend has it that Bellamy made the captain of the whaleship serve as pilot aboard the pirate flagship, the *Whidah*, and that the captain deliberately ran them all on the beach in a snowstorm. Apparently, however, the whaling skipper was not aboard the *Whidah* at all. What seems to have happened is that only a few days earlier the pirates had captured a coastwise sloop loaded with fine wines. On a dark, cold, snowy night who could resist having a little of the loot to warm the blood? The wine was distributed among the pirate ships, and everyone warmed his blood until no one could see where he was going. Almost the entire fleet piled up on the Cape Cod beach.

Only seven of the pirates survived. Captain Bellamy was one of them. He lived long enough to be arrested, taken up to Boston, tried, found guilty and hanged by the neck until dead.

It is a sure thing that Captain Bartholomew Roberts would not have made so stupid a mistake as Bellamy's. In fact, Captain Roberts allowed no drinking at all aboard his ship. That is, he tried to outlaw drinking. Of course there was some on the sly. But any pirate caught drinking by Captain Roberts was unceremoniously dumped over the side.

Roberts had other customs unusual for a pirate. He observed the Sabbath strictly. No fighting was done on Sunday, and all lights were doused even earlier than on week nights when all lights were out by eight o'clock. No gambling was permitted aboard Roberts' ship, and a strong watch was put over all prisoners to protect them, especially lady prisoners.

For battle, Roberts dressed in a damask waistcoat and breeches, with a silk sling over his shoulder to hold two pistols. He was an expert swordsman, especially with the razor-sharp cutlass which he favored. He also wore a red feather in his cap and a gold chain around his neck with a large diamond cross hanging from it.

Bartholomew Roberts had been a member of a pirate crew only six weeks. Then on the death of his captain, he was elected by the crew to fill the post. This was rapid advancement, but it proved to be recognition of piratical genius. For Captain Bartholomew Roberts was the most successful pirate who ever lived. In his career, which actually lasted a little more than two years, he captured more than four hundred ships. This record was unmatched by any other pirate in history.

Roberts' course ranged all over the Atlantic, from England to South America to the West Indies to Newfoundland to the African coast, where finally, on the morning of February 10, 1722, he was run to ground. A man-of-war caught him at anchor in a harbor, eating his breakfast. At the cry of the lookout, he cut his anchor cable and tried to fight his way out of the trap. He was overpowered.

Bartholomew Roberts had always made his crew promise that if he were killed they would throw his body, still dressed in the damask waistcoat and breeches, into the sea. The battle was going hotly when a round of grapeshot sliced into his throat, almost cutting off his head. A few minutes later, just before striking their pirate flag, Roberts' crew tossed over the side the still-bleeding body of history's most successful pirate.

The successes of Captain William Fly did not approach those of Captain Roberts. But Fly managed to make his end almost as dramatic. After plaguing the coast from North Carolina to New England, he was finally caught and taken to Boston, where he was speedily tried and convicted. He went to the gallows bravely, waving and smiling to the crowd which always assembled for hangings. He showed off to all the traditional nosegay of wild flowers in his

As the man-of-war approached, the lookout screamed.

bound hands and the gay bits of colored string
he had tied to his sleeves. It was a more somber
Captain Fly whom sailors saw next day: a body
hung in chains on one of the islands in Boston
Harbor, a warning to others not to try the career of Captain Fly.

Still men continued to try the career of piracy —not only men but women as well. The two most famous women pirates were Mary Read and Anne Bonny. Both came from England, and both wound up on the island of New Providence, the pirate capital of the New World. Both masqueraded as men in order to go a-pirating. The first, Mary Read, found herself on a pirate ship by mistake, when the sloop she was traveling on became a pirate's prize. The second, Anne Bonny, was already aboard the same pirate ship, voluntarily. She was in love with the pirate captain, had become his wife and was masquerading as a man in order to keep the superstitious crew from rebelling against having a woman aboard.

The victim, Mary Read, was in man's clothes serving before the mast because she was unable to pay her way across the Atlantic. Now she found pirating so much more exciting than the life of an ordinary seaman that she volunteered to join the pirate crew.

The relationship between the pirate captain and his wife was similar to that of Captain Cobham and Maria. The pirate captain, nicknamed "Calico Jack" Rackam because of his liking for calico trousers, had enough of piracy long before Anne was ready to give it up. In fact, after she had been ashore for a few months having their baby, she was ready to go right back to sea. Indeed, she left her baby and never returned to it again.

So it was that Rackam's oddly-assorted pirate crew was cruising off the coast of Jamaica one day in October, 1720, when a warship came rushing down on them. The crew fought well, but they were finally overcome by sheer weight of attackers. The last two pirates fighting on deck were Mary Read and Anne Bonny.

In the trial that followed, in Port Royal, Jamaica, both girls publicly announced their real sex. It then developed that Captain Rackam had known about Mary Read and had in fact married her to one of his crew. Not only that, but each girl was about to have a baby.

For that reason, both women were freed by the court. The men, including Rackam, were sentenced to death. Neither girl showed any signs of repentance. When asked if she were sorry for the life she had led, Mary Read replied no, and added that she was in favor of death for piracy. Without the threat of the noose, she explained, every fool would turn pirate and spoil the business for the experts. As for Anne Bonny, her attitude was demonstrated when she had her last meeting with Calico Jack Rackam.

He had been asked what his last request would be. He had said that he wanted to see his wife once more. It must have been a moving sight—the great iron door to Anne's cell creaking open, the shuffling, manacled man who had once been such a dashing figure silhouetted against the light behind the door. What the scene actually looked like has been lost in history. But we do know what Anne said.

She said, "I'm sorry to see you come to this." Then she added with a sneer: "If you had fought like a man, you need not have died like a dog."

Calico Jack said nothing. He turned and stumbled out to where the guards were waiting for him, to lead him to the scaffold and the hangman's rope.

Calico Jack Rackam might not have marched to the gallows if Anne had not talked him out of giving up piracy when he had wanted to a few years earlier. There are many accounts of pirates who quit as soon as they had made enough money to satisfy themselves. It would be nice to report that crime never paid in piracy and that sooner or later all pirates were punished for their lawlessness. But many pirates were not. We know of hundreds who "retired" and enjoyed their plunder without ever having to account for it.

This was especially true during the years when the British government tried the "King's Amnesty" method of stopping piracy, as we have seen in the chapters on Blackbeard and Bonnet. Sometimes local officials were bribed or an ex-pirate managed to hide his trail. Perhaps, in some cases, nobody happened to care. Whatever the reason, there were cases of an old renegade who would settle down happily with the proceeds of a few rich cruises and enjoy his illegal wealth for the rest of his life. But every once in a while there occurred an incident which proved that there is some justice in the world after all. Such an incident was the case of Captain Thomas Tew.

He had started as a privateersman out of Bermuda. Many a pirate began his career that way. Privateering was legal because each ship was licensed by its government to hunt down and attack the ships of other nations with which they were at war. But peace made privateering illegal, and the privateersmen were thrown out of work. Many decided to keep it up anyway and thus became pirates. That is what Thomas Tew did.

After taking a few merchant vessels in the Caribbean, he sailed to the Indian Ocean and went after some of the really rich prizes of the great Mocha Fleet, the ships that carried the treasures of India across to the Red Sea and Arabia. The first one he captured was so laden with gold and jewels that he needed to capture no more. Returning around the Cape of Good Hope and across the Atlantic, Tew and his men put into the harbor at Newport, Rhode Island, and divided the spoils. For Captain Tew there was a large enough share so that he could retire for the rest of his life. He bought a mansion overlooking Narragansett Bay and settled down to enjoy himself.

Not all of Tew's men were as thrifty as he. Within a few months most of them had squandered their wealth. Soon they were gathering in little groups and talking about going out after another of these rich Mocha frigates. When they called on Captain Tew and suggested it to him, he told them to go ahead if they wanted to, but to leave him out of it.

That was not at all what they had in mind. Most of Tew's men were convinced that he led some kind of charmed life. They were sure that only with him in command could they have as successful a cruise as the last one. They collected more than half of the old crew and descended on him again. When they explained that only he would bring them the luck they needed,

Tew agreed that they had indeed been lucky last time. But he tried to point out that perhaps they had used up their luck, and that they would never be so fortunate on another cruise. In fact, on this one they might pay for the luck of the last.

But his men would not agree. And they pleaded so convincingly and so long that he finally gave in. He would take them out once again, he said, but only this once. If they threw their money away after this cruise, they could starve for all he cared. This was absolutely the last time.

Off they sailed for the rich hunting grounds of the Indian Ocean. At the entrance to the Red Sea, they lay in wait for the first Mocha ship to come through. With them waited another pirate ship. Her captain was one Henry Every, another lucky pirate.

The Mocha fleet captains well knew by this time that they had to run the gantlet at the Red Sea entrance. So they collected in a convoy for the voyage back to India. They waited for night for the dash into the open ocean, and they almost slipped by without being noticed.

But the wind was not quite strong enough for the two slowest ships in the fleet. When dawn came, they were spotted by the pirates' lookouts, just before they got over the horizon.

Captain Tew was the first to catch up with them. He picked out the bigger one of the two, knowing that the Mocha ships were always lightly armed no matter how big. This time he was wrong.

The ship was the *Fateh Mahomed,* and she carried a whole row of heavy guns on each side. As Tew's ship approached, one row gave him a booming broadside. A jagged piece of metal struck Tew in the midriff. It ripped open his stomach and sent him spinning against the deckhouse.

The men who had talked Captain Tew into the cruise and who counted on his luck to bring them success were overwhelmed by the sight of him as he bled to death on the deck. They did not try to answer the *Fateh Mahomed*'s broadside or run up to grapple her. The helmsman let the pirate ship fall off on another tack, as

Tew's men carried him below to his cabin. There he died.

None of the crew was even injured by the broadside. It was only Captain Tew whose luck ran out.

Luck still favored the other pirate captain in the battle. Henry Every (sometimes referred to as John Avery) came up on the *Fateh Mahomed* while she was firing on Tew's ship. In a short exchange Every silenced her guns and forced her captain to surrender. Not only did he capture the *Fateh Mahomed*, but he also ran down on the second ship and engaged her.

She turned out to be the *Gunsway*, one of the richest ships in the entire fleet of India's Great Mogul. On this voyage the *Gunsway* carried an aunt of the Great Mogul, on a pilgrimage to Mecca. She was accompanied by dozens of attendants, and she carried with her a fabulous collection of jewels. Every and his crew slaughtered the *Gunsway*'s crew, the attendants and the Mogul's aunt, and made off with what today would amount to about a million dollars.

The pirates crossed the Atlantic to the West

A jagged piece of metal struck Captain Tew in the midriff.

Indies, where they put into the harbor of New Providence for a gigantic celebration. Some of them stayed in the West Indies. Every and a few of his shipmates went back to England. But they went cautiously; they had heard of the repercussions from their great capture.

When the news reached India, there were riots in which a number of Britons were killed. The Great Mogul arrested most of the representatives of the East India Company, the Englishmen who did business with India, and had them thrown in a dungeon. The British government apologized to the Great Mogul and offered a reward of £500 for each man in Every's crew. The East India Company doubled the reward.

Every and his shipmates went ashore in Ireland to see if the coast was clear. It was not. Almost immediately most of his companions were caught. They were taken to London, tried and hanged. Within a few weeks all had been rounded up except Every himself.

He changed his name to Bridgeman. He sneaked down into England and hid out in a small seacoast town in Devon. Cautiously he tried to convert his share of the loot into cash. This was difficult. Not only was all England on the lookout for Every and his pirates, but descriptions of the Great Mogul's jewels had been posted everywhere. And besides the reward notices, novels, songs and plays had been written about the "arch pirate." Every was one of the most famous men in England.

He found a friend he could trust and sent word to a few merchants in Bristol who were known to have had dealings with pirates before. A delegation called on him in his little cottage. They could not hide their amazement at the value of the jewels Every had. They assured him that they could sell them for a great deal of money, given plenty of time to pass them slowly into the market. They gave Every a big down payment and took most of the jewels back to Bristol with them.

Every was left to wait and to worry. Certainly he knew that he should not trust the Bristol merchants with such valuable jewels. But he had no alternative. Only through them could he convert his loot into money.

Days turned into weeks. After more than a month Every had spent the cash they had given him. He wrote to ask when he could expect his full payment. They sent him a little more money. He spent that. They sent him a few more pounds. When that was gone, his letters to Bristol went unanswered. Every took a chance and went to Bristol to confront the merchants.

They told him that they were paying him as much as they could and that it might take years to unload the jewels without exciting suspicion. Every demanded either more money or his jewels. The merchants refused. Every threatened to expose them. They reminded him that if he did, they might be arrested or fined; but he would be hanged.

Every gave up and returned to his little cottage. The merchants did no more than send him a few pounds now and then. He did not even have enough to pay the rent on the cottage so was thrown out. For a few months he begged in the streets. Then he became ill and died. He was buried at town expense without a coffin.

It was not until some years later, when one of the Great Mogul's jewels was traced back to the Bristol merchants, that England learned the ironic fate of Henry Every, the "arch pirate."

6

Pesthole of the Americas

You have probably noticed by now that the name of one place has cropped up again and again. The place is the island of New Providence. It was to New Providence that the crew of Captain James Flood insisted on going for a celebration after their rich cruise. It was New Providence that Blackbeard left when he went out on his last expedition. It was New Providence that Bonnet and his boys were heading for when they had the misfortune to cross paths with Blackbeard.

Henry Every put in at New Providence after his famous capture of the Great Mogul's ship *Gunsway*. Calico Jack Rackam preferred New Providence to most other places. So did his wife, Anne Bonny. So did Bartholomew Roberts, Ben Hornigold and more pirates than anyone could count. New Providence, now better known as Nassau, is one of the most beautiful islands on earth. But that is not why the pirates liked it so much.

It was perfectly situated, in the center of the group of islands which lay athwart the main trade routes from South America to Europe. Richest of the ships that sailed these routes were the great Plate Fleets of Spain. These were ships that came regularly from Spain to the South American ports, where their holds were loaded with treasures, including valuable silver plate, from the fabulous mines of South America. Then they sailed for home.

Look at the map and you will see how the Plate Fleets had to run the pirate gantlet. They could try to slip through the Straits of Florida. But often they were waylaid by pirates lying in

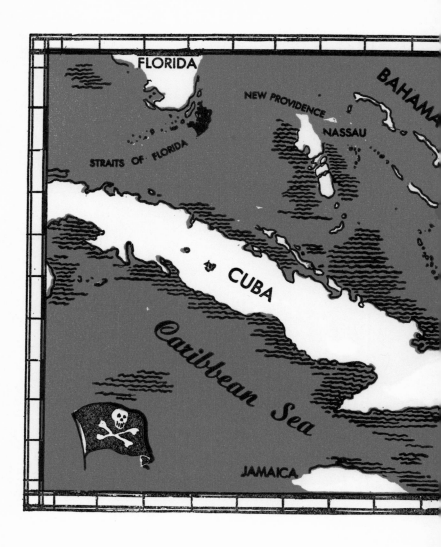

wait at the Bahama keys, just a day's sail from New Providence. Or the fleet could try to go south of the Bahama Islands by sailing through the Windward Passage, between Cuba and Hispaniola (the island which is now Haiti and the Dominican Republic). On this route they could be ambushed by pirates who ran down to Great Inagua Island or the Caicos Islands, only a few days' sail from New Providence. No wonder that in the New World all pirates' sea roads ran to New Providence.

No wonder too that, with such a strategic location, New Providence became the wildest frontier town in the New World. In earlier days it had been settled by law-abiding people. But in the continual war between England and Spain over all the West Indies, the English settlers had been driven off the island. Before anyone else could settle on it, the pirates took it over. They formed their own community, with their own laws—which amounted to no laws except those of pistol and cutlass. They had no legally elected officials; the town was run by the man who could beat up the most fellow pirates.

Day and night with no letup, New Providence was one riotous brawl. More pirates regularly arrived to celebrate their victories before the last ones had spent all their money and gone off to sea again. The worst towns of the American Wild West had nothing on New Providence. The island was described perfectly by the governor of Bermuda, a thousand miles away. He called it a "nest of infamous rascals."

Partly in order to clean out New Providence, the British government decided to declare the "King's Amnesty." Early in 1718 a copy of the proclamation was brought into the harbor by His Majesty's Ship *Phenix*. The captain went ashore and read it to the pirates who gathered around him. They ushered him back to his boat and sent him on his way. A month later he tried again. He was sent on his way again, a little less politely this time. In his report to London he wrote that the inhabitants of New Providence "showed no small hatred to government."

That was the situation a few months later when a new governor of the island, appointed by the king's ministers in England, arrived to take charge. His name was Woodes Rogers. Scarcely anyone would have bet that he could restore order on the island—scarcely anyone, that is, except those who knew Woodes Rogers well.

He was already famous at home as one of England's great captain adventurers. Ten years earlier he had sailed around the world, something that only a few men had done at that time. Besides capturing Spanish galleons, which he was licensed to do by his government, Rogers also rescued a shipwrecked sailor from the Juan Fernandez Islands. The sailor's name was Alexander Selkirk, and his story became famous in Daniel Defoe's *Robinson Crusoe*. Woodes Rogers was an adventurous man and a brave one, and he did not expect his new job to be a picnic. He did not realize, though, how tough it really would be.

Rogers arrived off the entrance to New Providence harbor with three vessels, the *Rose*, the *Milford* and the *Delicia*, his flagship. Dusk was settling over the island and he did not know the channel into the harbor, so he decided to wait out in the roadstead until morning. He ordered the *Milford* to run down to the second entrance to the harbor and blockade it. With the *Rose* and the *Delicia* he anchored outside the larger entrance. He now had the harbor bottled up, on the theory that some of the pirates had probably guessed who he was and might try to make a run for it.

They had indeed guessed who he was. But only one or two pirates had decided to attempt an escape. The most determined one was a pirate named Charles Vane. He had only just arrived in the harbor with a cargo of fine wines and brandy, and he had no intention of letting the new governor take it away from him. Vane chose to try a dash for the open sea, and he devised an ingenious way to make his escape.

Outside the harbor entrance Woodes Rogers waited for dawn. In the distance he could hear the normal din of life in the town. The harbor was quiet except for an occasional thump of a rolling cask or the slap-slap of loosened rigging. At the harbor entrance the *Rose* and the *Delicia* creaked on their anchor cables. On the

decks of the two warships, the members of the
night watch murmured to themselves. The only
other sound in the darkness was the lap-lap of
the water against the anchored bows as the tide
ran out of New Providence harbor. Then the
night blew up.

An exploding, burning brigantine came racing down the channel toward the harbor entrance. In the light of the flames roaring into
her lower sails, it could be seen that her wheel
was tied down. She was running before the
wind and burning wildly as she came. She had
been set afire, with no one aboard, and aimed
for the warship guarding the harbor mouth. She
had been aimed well because she was headed
straight for the *Rose*, lying at anchor across the
channel.

The captain of the *Rose* only had time to
yell for the anchor cable to be cut. Frantically
the *Rose*'s sailors cracked on sail to swing out
of the way. There was no room to maneuver
in the narrow entrance way, and all the *Rose*
could do was flee before the pursuing fire ship.
Fortunately the trade wind was so strong that

she could get under way in time, and she just
made it to open sea before the burning brigantine raced out of the harbor. As the fire ship
sailed by, the captain of the *Rose,* and Woodes
Rogers aboard the *Delicia* a few hundred yards
away, could make out a darkened sloop just behind her. The sloop's deck was filled with pirates, cheering as they ran to the safety of the
open ocean.

Rogers was tempted to chase them. But in the
darkness they could easily lead him onto one
of the thousands of uncharted coral reefs. And
if his ships were lured away from the harbor,
many of the other pirates could escape too. He
watched the flaming decoy burn to the water's
edge. Then he settled down to wait for morning.

He did not know that few of the other pirates
had any intention of making a break for it.
They had, they figured, a much better idea.
They planned to "surrender," accept the King's
Amnesty and then, little by little, resume control of the island by taking Rogers in as one
of them. Previous governors had been bribed

The burning brigantine raced toward the warship.

into letting the pirates run the island their own
way, and the pirates naturally assumed that
Woodes Rogers could be bought just as easily
as the others.

That is why Rogers received, on that June

The captain of the Rose ordered the anchor cable cut.

morning in 1718, a welcome that came as quite
a surprise after the incident of the night before.
No sooner had he stepped ashore than he was
met by an informal reception committee. Probably there never was a more raffish looking recep-

tion committee in the history of the Americas, even including some of the Indians who met the first settlers. The members of the pirate delegation wore tattered shirts and trousers, probably unwashed since the time they were new, and that must have been ages before. Their boots were caked with mud, scarred by coral and streaked with the blood of countless battles. One pirate wore rings in his ears. Another had a patch over one eye. Most of them had scraggly beards, stained brown by chewing tobacco. Each man tried to hold himself erect and dignified in the reception line. They stood in silence as the new governor walked up the wharf.

The leader of the delegation stepped forward and recited a speech of welcome. Rogers thanked him. He was glad to be here, he said. He had come to perform two important duties. One was to establish law and order on the island. The other duty was to accept formally the surrender of any pirates who wished to turn themselves in. For a few days any pirate could surrender, swear that he would never turn to piracy again, and that would be that. There would be no

punishment, so long as the man remained a reformed pirate. This offer, of course, could hold
only for a few days. After that . . . Governor
Rogers looked meaningly at the marines standing beside him.

Considering the affair at the mouth of the
harbor the night before, imagine Woodes Rogers' surprise to see all the pirates around the
wharf obediently form a line and march up to
him. One by one they came to swear that they
were through with piracy and would never again
indulge in the dirty business. As the first few
stepped up and delivered the same set speech,
Rogers thought it was some kind of trick. Then
he noticed that Henry Jennings, one of the pirate captains, had gathered a band of musket-
wielding men who were herding the pirate-con-
fessors into line. Rogers realized that Jennings
was handing over nearly the entire pirate population to him. He began to wonder what the
price would be.

He did not have to wait long to find out.
Within a few days of his arrival the first propo-
sition was put to him. The pirate who called

on the Governor did not identify himself, but
there could be little doubt that he was speaking
for most of the island's inhabitants. The caller
explained that he and his friends were more
than happy to go along with Rogers' plan. If
the authorities back in England thought that
New Providence had turned honest, there might
be fewer warships hanging around the ap-
proaches to the island, and it would be a lot
safer for the pirates to come and go about their
business. Whatever the Governor wanted them
to do to keep up the appearance of having reformed, they would do. Of course, they could
not actually give up piracy. But they would
gladly *pretend* that they had, in order to fool
the King's ministers. Not only that, but they
were prepared to raise the Governor's share of
the plunder from the former governor's eight
per cent to ten per cent.

Now of course, the caller went on, since the
pirates were prepared to go that far, they expected a bit of protection in return. If the waters around the Bahamas were still going to be
invaded by His Majesty's warships, the pirates

were not sure that they could afford to continue to pay Rogers his full ten per cent. They had had trouble with some of the previous governors on this score, the pirate explained. But he could see that Rogers was an honest man who would live up to his side of a bargain. Before the caller could get a chance to ask whether or not Rogers agreed, the Governor had recovered from his astonishment and the pirate had been shown to the door.

In the meeting that took place in one of the taverns a few hours later, there was some difference of opinion among the pirates. A few of the impatient ones were ready to march on the Governor's house, shoot up his guards, put Rogers aboard his ship and escort it out of the harbor, with a warning not to return. But a majority listened to the argument of Captain Jennings: give the Governor a bit more time and try again. He might take a little longer, but he would come around just as all the rest had. If they drove him off now, the King's ministers might really get angry and send an invasion force to storm the island and capture all the pirates.

Those who were caught would be hanged. Those who got away probably would not be able to retake the island. It would be smarter to wait and enjoy a few more weeks of rest. Besides, they had nothing to lose by waiting.

That was where Captain Henry Jennings was completely wrong. For in those few weeks of respite granted to him, Woodes Rogers started his campaign to clean up New Providence Island. Jennings and his pirates did not know it at the time, of course, but their days as pirates were numbered by those very weeks they gave to Rogers.

The Governor did not have enough troops to enforce his authority on the island. Those pirates who argued that they should storm his house were correct in guessing that they could have done so successfully. Rogers had arrived with three ships. He had allowed only a few of his men to come ashore, so that his whole force could not be counted by the pirates. Meanwhile he hinted darkly at the huge "army" of men he kept aboard his ships in the harbor. Actually there were very few. Even that force dwindled to almost nothing a few days after his arrival.

The captains of two of his ships were under orders to support Rogers until he was established. Although the Governor argued that he was far from established, the captains decided that he was. So they put out to sea and headed south to Jamaica. Rogers continued to refer to the army of men aboard his one ship still in the harbor. But he would have been defenseless against the combined numbers of the pirates if they had all risen against him. Without enough military force, he could only use persuasion—an unlikely weapon against this mob. But he did try it, and he was successful. This is how he did it.

First, he started one of history's first land reform campaigns. In the lawless, ungoverned, nearly uncivilized community of New Providence, no one owned any land, or anything else for that matter, if someone stronger took it away from him. Now Woodes Rogers tried what seemed at the outset to be a ridiculous strategy. He divided the island into 2000-foot-square lots and gave the lots to the pirates.

The first reaction, after surprise, was amusement. What would any of the pirates want with a piece of land when they could pitch a sailcloth tent anywhere they wanted? And who was to clean up and build on his lot (one of the stipulations of the program), especially those lots in the bush back of the town, when he was perfectly happy in the swarm of tents near the water? For the first few days the Governor's land reform program amounted to little more than providing the subject for jokes in the taverns.

But the pirates did not yet appreciate Woodes Rogers' real genius. He was not giving away just lots. With each lot he also gave away a formal, impressive piece of parchment. It was a deed, he explained, and it meant that the piece of land described on it legally belonged to the man who had the piece of parchment. The deed gave the owner full right to the land and anything on it (or any treasure buried under it), and the right to keep everyone else off it if he wanted.

Pirates asked to see a deed and have it read to them.

The strategy worked exactly as Rogers had planned. At first a few pirates came around to the Governor's office, asking to see what a deed looked like and to have it read to them. Then a few accepted their pieces of land. As more and more of them started showing off their impressive parchment documents in the taverns, it became a fad to have one. Soon

nearly every pirate had his piece of parchment, entitling him to a plot of ground on the
island. Then nature took its course.

One pirate lost his parchment to another
at the gambling table. He went to Rogers
and asked for another lot. Rogers said no; there
could be only one lot per man, and the records
showed that this man already had his. Further-
more the man who had won the lot was forced
to return it. While being lax about some of
the other laws for the time being, Rogers en-
forced this one strictly. Within a few days each
pirate owned a single lot—and had begun to get
the idea.

One by one, trying to do it when no one else
noticed, each pirate sneaked out of town and
went to look over his lot. The first sight of the
work that would be required to make it livable
sent him right back to town. But soon he was
back again, studying the contours and the out-
lines of his land, realizing that it was all his, to
do with as he wanted. A change of heart began
to come over him. In the shiftless, spendthrift,
insecure life he had been leading, here was the

first thing he could cling to as his own. No officer of His Majesty's Navy, no admiralty judge could claim that it really belonged to someone else. It belonged only to the man with the legal, impressive bit of parchment. And nobody else could take it away from him. Suddenly a band of profligate vagabonds was converted into a community of landowners. And then Woodes Rogers applied the second part of his strategy.

There was only one group for whom the New Providence pirates nourished a built-in hatred more than His Majesty's sailors and officers of the crown. That was the Spaniards. The history of the New World in those years is a history of Englishmen and Spaniards fighting for it. There were plenty of Spanish pirates. But the ones who lived on New Providence at this time were mainly of English origin. And they regarded Spaniards with a consuming hate.

Warfare in the eighteenth century did not involve the callous slaughter of thousands, including noncombatants, as warfare does in the twentieth century. But its hand-to-hand battles were brutal enough. And the ingenious tortures for prisoners developed by the eighteenth century armies, Spanish and English alike, made the tortures of the American Indians seem mild. As a result, nothing turned a New Providence pirate's blood cold more quickly than the mention of an invasion by the Spaniards.

Woodes Rogers knew this well. There is nothing in the records to prove it, but it seems likely that he was thinking of the Spaniards all the time when he was handing out pieces of land to the New Providence pirates. As soon as the pirates became fascinated with the fact that they owned their own land, Governor Rogers started warning them about the possibility of a Spanish invasion. Ordinarily such a warning would have made little impression. The pirates had their own ships. There were two entrances to the New Providence harbor. It would be a simple enough matter to crowd on sail and clear out before the Spaniards landed, and then come back after the trouble was over. The Spaniards had captured New Providence once before; they had stayed only a few years before going on their way.

But the pirates looked at such an invasion differently now. If the Spaniards came, they would be taking over all the land which belonged to the pirates. Now instead of choosing whether to fight on land or sea, the pirates would be forced to fight on land to defend their rightful property. No longer could they fight or run as they chose. Now they would be defending their own soil.

As the pirates reacted the way Rogers had figured they would, he put them to work. New Providence then had one big fort overlooking the main entrance to the harbor. But it had fallen into ruins. Rogers set the pirates to work repairing it. The work did not go very smoothly at first, because the pirate workmen found that lifting blocks of stone employed quite different muscles from the ones which swung a cutlass. Also, there was a good bit of revelry on the job. But under almost constant supervision by Rogers the big fort was repaired. It was time for the next move in the Governor's strategy.

Some months had gone by. Understandably many of the pirates were thirsting to get back

to sea again. More visitors like the first one had
come to Rogers' office. The boys were getting
awfully anxious to do a little more pirating,
they argued. Everyone agreed that New Providence was becoming a nicer place. The tents
had been replaced by palm-thatched huts. The
streets were streets instead of the open sewers
they had been when Rogers arrived. Many of
the private plots had been improved and built
on. But the "commerce" of the island, the business that kept it alive, had been dead too long.
If a few of the ships could not go out soon and
bring in some more loot, everyone would begin to get hungry. Rogers had an answer for
this problem, and he put it into effect.

Since there was always the danger of an
attack by the Spaniards, whether war between
England and Spain had been officially declared
or not, Rogers could legally license his reformed
pirates to become privateers. That is, he could
grant them licenses to arm their ships and go in
search of Spanish vessels. The license entitled
them to capture and loot any Spanish warship

or merchantman. The Governor started issuing the licenses. Happily the former pirates lined up for their permits and signed up their crews. One by one the pirate ships weighed anchor and sailed out of the harbor again. This time they were licensed to chase, kill and plunder only the Spaniards.

Therein lay the danger. Once the "reformed" pirates got to sea again, a few of them found it impossible to resist the temptation to chase the first ship they found, Spanish or not. That was the difference between privateering and piracy. And it presented the first really big challenge to the leadership of Governor Rogers.

As soon as he received the news of the first pirate crew reverting to its old business, Rogers sent for the most famous pirate on the island. Ben Hornigold, you will remember, was the man who schooled Blackbeard. When Woodes Rogers started to clean up New Providence, Hornigold went along with the cleanup, agreeing with Jennings that sooner or later the pirates and Rogers could make a deal. Now

Rogers offered him one. It was not exactly the kind of deal Hornigold and Jennings had had in mind, but it was interesting nevertheless.

Rogers seemed to be more worried about the loathed Spaniards than about the men who had just turned pirate again. He pointed out to Hornigold that if the Spaniards were watching developments on New Providence at all, they must have been unhappy at the way things were going. They would have seen the repair of the fort, the forming of a pirate defense force, the licensing of the privateers and all the improvements.

But now the Spaniards must be happy to see some of the men reverting to piracy. A thing like that could catch on, Rogers pointed out. If these fellows got away with it, more and more of the New Providence inhabitants would turn pirate again. And where would their navy of privateers go?

Also, those who turned pirate certainly could not come back to New Providence without being arrested. That meant that for every crew turned pirate the defenses of the island were reduced by one more ship. If this went on, all the Spaniards would have to do would be to lie in wait. As soon as the defenses were reduced sufficiently, the enemy could strike. With most of the island's best fighters gone, New Providence could not hold out for long. And if Ben Hornigold thought there was no fate worse than being hanged as a pirate, he should think for a moment of his fate as a prisoner of the fiendish Spaniards.

Hornigold did not have to think long. He had a suggestion; he would go himself in chase of the crew that had turned pirate. He would bring them in and hand them over for punishment. Rogers waited a moment to pretend that the idea had never occurred to him. Then he and Hornigold shook hands on it, and Hornigold received a commission to chase down the pirates.

So it was that Woodes Rogers converted Ben Hornigold, one of the founders of piracy in the New World, into becoming a pirate chaser. It was one of the most impressive accomplishments in the history of the Americas. And it was a

major turning point in the establishment of law
and order in the New World.

Hornigold found his men. He brought them
in and turned them over to Rogers. The Governor then employed another step in his plan. He
had appointed a cabinet of counselors, most of
them reformed pirates. He called them before
him for advice on his next move.

These renegades, he explained, should be
punished, not only because they had broken
their solemn word not to revert to piracy, but
also to serve as a warning to any others who
were contemplating the same move. Should the
men be tried or not?

What could his cabinet of former pirates say?
The renegades were ordered to be tried.

There were ten of them. All were found
guilty. All were hanged—except one. Governor
Rogers announced that because there was some
slight doubt in his mind about the guilt of this
one, he was pardoned. So it was that all over
New Providence men repeated the lesson to
each other. If you turn pirate again, you will
be caught and hanged. If you play along with

the Governor, as Hornigold did, you can become one of the Governor's trusted aides. And
no one could praise the Governor's fairness
more loudly than the one pirate who had been
pardoned. Woodes Rogers thought of everything.

That is why, when the long-threatened Spanish invasion finally did come, in February of
1720, the inhabitants of New Providence were
ready for it. The Spaniards came in a huge
force, landing from eleven ships. Two thousand attackers, of whom 1,400 were army reg-
ulars, marched on the town. They outnumbered
the island's defenders by more than two to one.

And they were beaten off. No record has yet
been discovered which gives the details of the
battle. Perhaps Rogers, Hornigold or Jennings
worked out some ingenious strategy of defense
which outflanked or ambushed the attackers.
Perhaps it was simply that the former pirates
were fighting as never before and on land as the
Spaniards never expected they would do.

In any case, the successful defense of New
Providence shows how much had been accom-

The Governor announced the turncoats would be hanged.

plished in less than two years. Governor Woodes Rogers had landed on the island on a June morning in 1718. He had found a squalid tent city more lawless than any in the New World.

He had transformed it into an orderly community with an effective defense force. He had found the scurviest band of cutthroats in the Western Hemisphere. He had transformed them into a lawful, loyal group of followers who served as his advisers, chased down pirates and fought off an invasion that outnumbered them two to one.

So it was that New Providence, once the pesthole of the Americas, was turned into a peaceful, law-abiding town. And with the reform of New Providence, the great days of piracy in the New World died out. Other forces contributed to this development. But to Woodes Rogers must go a huge share of the credit for putting an end to the almost unrestricted piracy which had plagued the seas around the Americas for more than two centuries.

If you ever go to what is now Nassau, the capital of the Bahamas Islands, off the eastern coast of Florida, take a walk up the slanting road where the Front Street traffic winds around the big British Colonial Hotel. There is a church at the corner. In its graveyard lie the remains of Governor Woodes Rogers. He died in office in 1732. And he is buried on the island he always loved. There is a simple headstone, but it stands for a great deal. It marks the final resting place of a man little mentioned in your history books but one of the greatest figures in the civilization of the New World.

Index